~~Always a Bridesmaid~~

Finally the Bride

A memoir about
finding love
after walking
down everyone
else's aisle

JEN GLANTZ

Author of *Always a Bridesmaid (For Hire)*

Finally the Bride: A Memoir About Finding Love After Walking Down Everyone Else's Aisle

Copyright © 2025 by Jen Glantz. All rights reserved.

Published by For Gemma, Brooklyn, NY, USA

No part of this publication may be reproduced, stored in a retrieval system, or transmitted in any form or by any means, electronic, mechanical, photocopying, recording, or otherwise, without the prior written permission of the publisher.

Cover photo by Susan Shek
Graphics: Elena Platova

Paperback ISBN: 979-8-9921920-0-1
Ebook ISBN: 979-8-9921920-1-8

First Edition: 2025

This is a work of nonfiction. Names, characters, places, and incidents are based on the author's recollections and experiences. Certain names and identifying characteristics have been changed to protect the privacy of individuals.

The information in this book is provided for informational purposes only. The author and publisher make no representations or warranties concerning the accuracy or completeness of the contents of this work and specifically disclaim all warranties.

This book is for you, my dear stranger-friend. It's for the moments when you think nobody will ever understand what you're going through, for the times when everyone else's lives look like they belong in wall-hanging frames while yours looks like a finger-painted mess.

It's for anyone who wants to believe in the impossible but doesn't know how anymore.

Thank you for being here and for reading this story about how love found me when I swore I thought it never would.

Table of Contents

Preface 1

Chapter 1: You Will Never Find Love 7

Chapter 2: You Will Still Try to Find Love 16

Chapter 3: Sometimes It Doesn't Happen 21

Chapter 4: To Find One, First Find Many 32

Chapter 5: How to Mess up a Relationship 47

Chapter 6: It's Been an Adventure Getting Here 58

Chapter 7: Conversations You Have When You Get

    Engaged 63

Chapter 8: In Defense of Bridezillas 74

Chapter 9: Be My Guest 84

Chapter 10: My Big Fat Divorce 95

Chapter 11: I Don't Want to Be Your Friend Anymore 106

Chapter 12: Money Talks but I Talk Back 119

Chapter 13: How to Cancel Your Wedding 130

Chapter 14: And the Secret to Marriage Is 148

Chapter 15: The Saddest Bride I Ever Did See 160

Chapter 16: A Million More Tomorrows 168

Chapter 17: Silly Little Date 175

Chapter 18: Finally the Bride 185

Acknowledgments 188

About the Author 190

Preface

Hey, you! I'm Jen Glantz.

I'll skip to the good part. I got engaged to the love of my life in July of 2019.

He dug one knee into the sand and eyed me with a look of constipation—a look that said, "I am pushing for the right words, but nothing is coming out."

Eventually, he squeezed out a "Will you marry me?" and I screamed, "I've been waiting for this for six years, you dumb fool!"

The ring, thankfully, didn't get lost in the piles of beach sand.

But what happened after that is the really good part because, like most engaged people, I lost my freaking mind.

What nobody tells you is that after you have that ring on your finger, everyone treats you differently.

The nail technician will ask you personal questions like "Are you sure you're not making a mistake?" and you'll tell her, "Of course I'm making a mistake—who in this world should paint their nails neon yellow after getting engaged?" She'll caress your ring finger, raise one eyebrow, and correct herself: "Not that," as she twists the ring, "this."

Finally the Bride

Every single family member you share an ounce of DNA with will ask you when the wedding is and if they can bring their toy poodle or their new boyfriend or their ex-husband.

Your friends will cry tears—some happy for you, some sad that they are not you—and then ask if you want to go to Vegas or New Orleans or Mexico, or if we plan ahead and don't invite cheap Jessica, we could maybe even do Costa Rica!

Your parents will want to know logistics, dates, vendors, budgets, whether you've considered how hot it is to get married in Florida in June—that's the start of hurricane season.

While all of these questions are warranted, it's too much, too soon, and you will simply go insane.

I'm supposed to be an all-star wedding expert with years of experience helping complete strangers two-step down the aisle and say "I do," but the truth is, I'm not. I'm not a wedding planner. I never wanted to be involved in the wedding industry. I don't even like weddings.

But I love people. That's why I started Bridesmaid for Hire in 2014. Because weddings make people bonkers, and I'm the perfect sidekick to help those who feel like their life is scattered on the ground and desperately need someone by their side to help pick it all up.

Here's what you should know: in the past ten years, I've worked hundreds of weddings for strangers as their hired bridesmaid.

PREFACE

I have a closet full of bridesmaid dresses that would put the character from *27 Dresses* to shame. I've been to every version of a Chippendales performance ever created, and if Channing Tatum ever needs to hire a choreographer for the next *Magic Mike* sequel, I'm available.

My first wedding was for Ashley from Maple Grove, Minnesota, who, after firing her maid of honor, hired me to take her place. The job then took me all over: to Times Square for a wedding for two grooms from Australia who wanted to get married in the middle of the street; to Vegas for a surprise wedding that lasted four days; to Staten Island for a wedding that lasted four minutes; and to Kansas for a wedding that had me clicking my heels saying, "There's no place like home."

I've found myself on my hands and knees in bathrooms, lifting up layers of tulle and taffeta so the bride could pee without having her fairy-tale wedding dress come face-to-face with the murky toilet bowl water. I've spent countless Saturday afternoons at Kleinfeld's and David's Bridal helping brides find the dress of their dreams, and well over 2,000 hours on the phone with brides as far away as Turkey who were looking for advice. I've shared my stories with the *TODAY Show*, *Good Morning America*, *The Steve Harvey Show*, and *Nightline*; with *USA Today*, *NY Magazine*, *Business Insider*, *The Knot*, and *Elle* magazine.

Finally the Bride

When it comes to weddings, I've seen a lot.

I've seen more than one bride spill Diet Coke all over her pearly white dress minutes before walking down the aisle, and dozens of bridesmaids on wedding-day scavenger hunts in their Aldo heels, trying to hunt down the groom mere minutes before the ceremony. I've helped bring bridesmaids back to life after they drank too much the night before the wedding, and I've answered phone calls right in the middle of my REM cycle when a bride called at 4 AM because she had that nightmare again—the one where no one shows up to her wedding because the date on her invitation is wrong.

I've helped brides, mothers of brides, maids of honor, and hundreds of bridesmaids through my Bridesmaid Boot Camp Crash Course and Ask a Professional Bridesmaid column for *BRIDES* magazine. As just a perpetual bridesmaid, I've written hundreds of articles giving wedding advice to brides without ever being one myself.

When Adam and I got engaged, I had no idea what kind of wedding I wanted. So I asked everyone and was flushed with a Costco-sized grocery list of advice:

- "You should elope. Having a big wedding is stupid! Take the money and use it on a honeymoon."

- "You shouldn't even get married. What's marriage anyway? Also, no one ever really wants to go to a wedding."

- "You should have a big wedding! You'll regret it if you elope."

- "You should wear Spanx under your dress. It'll let you keep eating all that pizza you like before your big day!"

- "You should have five bridesmaids, not six! Oh! They should wear flower crowns. Flower crowns are so cool right now."

- "You should wait to get pregnant until after the wedding. You don't want to be pregnant at your own celebration!"

- "You really shouldn't get married in Florida in July. It'll be too hot! So hot."

- "You should do what you want! Don't listen to anyone else. But I will tell you, don't invite more than 100 people. Over 100 and your wedding will feel like a weekend at Club Med."

- "You should hire your own bridesmaids! Ha! Wouldn't that be so, so, so?" (Meta. It would be meta. And it's probably going to happen.)

So much advice that my head started to expand and my heart started to do backflips, as if to say: ENOUGH! FINE! OKAY, YOU WIN! YOU WIN YOU WIN YOU WIN.

Finally the Bride

But slowly, I started to realize that the more I let other people's opinions dictate my wedding, the more I lost myself in the whole process.

This isn't a story about love and weddings. It's a story about figuring out what you want in life and whom you want to live it with.

I want to tell it all to you, starting from the beginning, when an expert told me I was forever doomed in the love department—and I believed her.

Meet the *expert*, Danielle the psychic.

Chapter 1

YOU WILL NEVER FIND LOVE

There should be stars for great wars like ours.
There ought to be awards and plenty of
champagne for the survivors.
-Sandra Cisneros

It's my turn, so I sit down in front of a woman who looks like she raided the jewelry section of Forever 21.

"Come on, honey." Her hand flaps. "Speak! What question do you have?"

"Just one?" I ask, crumpling a napkin in my palm. On it, a long list of things I was hoping to get answers to.

The psychic's eyes boomerang. Behind me, the line of people waiting for her attention is getting longer. My time is getting shorter. I quit wasting it.

Career or love? Love or career? I wrestle both topics in my mind, desperate for help.

Finally the Bride

Those are the two areas of my life that haunt me like voicemails from robocallers and telemarketers. I don't want to answer, but that doesn't mean they still don't dial my number with questions.

Career! I scream in my head.

"Love!" I say out loud to the psychic. "Please tell me about my love life."

Sorry, career. I adore you, sometimes more than anything else. But in this moment, I need to know how much longer I'm going to be dining at a table for one, declining plus ones on wedding invitations.

"Current love?" she drawls, with a high-pitched, overexaggerated mystical accent that makes her stubborn New Jersey accent sound like a passport of all of the places in her life she's traveled to. "Or future love?"

"Come on! Shouldn't you know I don't have a current anything? Unless you count the guy at coat check who showed me his teeth when I handed him my jacket and yelled, 'Checkmate!' That's about as close to flirting as I get these days," I overshare.

I stop talking and shake my head. Who actually believes in psychics anyway? I don't think I do. But then again, I'm not too sure. I did wait in a 45-minute line, in 16-degree weather, to get into this Valentine's Day party for "Lonely Hearts" just

1. YOU WILL NEVER FIND LOVE

to get as many life answers as I could in this free 15-minute session.

What New Yorkers will do for cheap entertainment is bonkers.

But when it's jaw-clenchingly cold out, and you haven't left your apartment in four days, and you're afraid to spend your third Valentine's Day in a row sinking into the couch, binge-eating raw cookie dough and pity laughing at some '90s Meg Ryan rom-com, there's a refreshing kind of beauty in spending time with a stranger who may or may not have the power to tell you the game plan of your life.

I once met a woman who went to a psychic in the East Village and got the news that a year from that moment she'd meet a guy whose name started with the letter B and fall in love.

Two years later, inside a tequila-scented bar with a broken PAC-MAN machine, she told me about how she was engaged to a guy named Brian.

A little prediction, I thought, even if it was as spotty as a weatherperson predicting rain in Florida, was better than approaching this love thing totally blind.

"Take me to that psychic right now," I begged the woman from the bar that night. It was 3 am. We rang her psychic and twelve more. All of them were closed for the night, presumably off getting their supernatural beauty sleep.

Finally the Bride

Yet, here I am, six months later, sitting in front of a psychic named Diane, hoping she'll get to the point and tell me the guy's name will start with a Z or a P just so I can know that there is at least one guy out there I am destined to marry.

"I have bad news for you," the psychic says.

No, oh no, no. You never want to hear the following people say they have bad news for you: a doctor, a dry cleaner, or someone you love dearly. But perhaps the most confusing person to utter those words is a psychic.

No news, I imagined, is better than bad news. Ignorance is bliss, but when it comes to your heart, ignorance is all we have.

"Ha! You, honey, may never find love. Looks like you'll grow old and be miserable like me."

"Excuse me, Diane." I lean forward, my eyes like spotlights, wide open and bright. "Is this some kind of early April Fool's joke?"

"Looks like it's going to take a year for you to even be ready to find someone."

"A year?" I complain. "I'm ready now!" I swat my fist on her wobbly table. Her tarot cards do backflips, as if to say: Jen, we too are confused by this news.

"It doesn't matter," she says. "You need time."

"TIME! I DON'T NEED TIME!"

1. YOU WILL NEVER FIND LOVE

Behind me, people's ears are turned inward, their mouths smirking at my misfortune, counting their luck, realizing since I was given the curse of being loveless the odds must be in their favor.

"Until then, do things for yourself. Travel?"

My eyes splatter out tears.

"Oh, here is something interesting," she continues, though I wish she wouldn't.

She flips over a line of tarot cards. One with a dagger on it, another fire, and finally a crown.

"Go to Disneyland. That's what you should do."

I sit back in the chair. My face flushes. My heart punches. "Disneyland? Are you kidding me?"

Love is not some fairy tale, I know. The last guy I had goo-goo eyes for told me just weeks ago that he never wanted to see me again. So trust me, I know that real love isn't rainbows and butterflies.

But here I am, having a staring contest with psychic Diane, who is telling me that I'm supposed to go off and marry Mickey Mouse or ride Space Mountain and fall in love with the attendant who will clean up my post-rollercoaster puke.

"I wish I had better news for you," she mutters, rolling her wrist, signaling me to skedaddle. "But I don't! Next!"

"Oh," I say, doomed. The dagger, the fire, the crown, all stabbing my heart at once.

Finally the Bride

I get up, shake her hand, take her card, and flick it into the trash can.

Love isn't some fairy tale, Jen. Get over it!

I never will.

When I get up, I ask the woman at the bar who went before me if the psychic had given her a similar prescription.

"No! She said I'm going to meet my match at this party, so, umm, would you mind leaving me alone? I want to seem coy and available."

I back away, eyeing Diane and the next victim approaching her.

What scared me the most about my love diagnosis at the time was that it seemed right. For most of my twenties, I was single. The world knew about it, celebrated it, and put me on a pedestal for it.

I wrote hundreds of articles and essays about first dates with guys that would later have me running up quite the therapy bill. I penned an entire memoir about how all my friends were getting engaged and I couldn't even land a second date.

1. YOU WILL NEVER FIND LOVE

JDate, the dating app for Jewish singles, ran banner ads with my face on it, advertising the app as a place for people like "Jen Glantz: always single, always looking." A cousin tried to set me up with another cousin of ours, because, well, she felt I was running out of options (some days I agreed with her).

I went to matchmakers, had my mom manage my dating apps, and tried out for *The Bachelor* not once, not twice, but three times.

I should have believed the psychic. I should have woken up every morning and repeated her words like a mantra. But for some reason, I didn't. I couldn't help it—I still believed in love.

Four years after I'd sat across from Diane, I found her on the internet and sent her the email below. Why? When someone gives you advice, you say thank you, even if it's after the fact.

Because no matter how wrong it is, every sentence, every word, has the power to change us, even if we don't realize it.

Finally the Bride

Dearest Diane,

Years ago, on one of those cold New York City nights where it feels like your coat is evaporating into your skin, I met you at a singles' party, and you told me I probably would never find love. That I'd end up miserable, just like you. And the truth is, you were right. That girl you were looking at wasn't ready to find anything, let alone someone to be her soulmate. She was broken, lost, shown by men that fairy tales should have horror movie endings instead. She actually thought love was when you got good at hiding the weird things about yourself! Can you believe that, Diane? Me? Hide things!

But dearest Diane, you were also wrong. Because years of trying my luck on Tinder and nights eyeballing potentials I was too shy to say hello to at bars taught me this: love isn't something you find. Love isn't a pair of keys you lost in beach sand. It's not a fallen tooth you must find to impress the Tooth Fairy. It's not a receipt you think is in your glove compartment but isn't there when you want to return something at Bed Bath and Beyond. Love is something that comes many moments after you sit across from someone on a first date and think, "Whoa, this person has held my attention almost as much as an episode of Game of Thrones.*"*

1. YOU WILL NEVER FIND LOVE

Well, I just want to say thank you, because I know if you told me that love was around the corner, I would have spent a long time looking for it in all the wrong places and maybe never would have found it, because what I needed was a kick in the butt to work a little harder on myself first. Frankly, I needed to get off my butt and leave the broken, scared and stomped-on parts of my heart behind. Thank you for helping me do that, Diane.

-Jen Glantz

P.S. You probably already knew all of this, didn't you?

Chapter 2
YOU WILL STILL TRY TO FIND LOVE

I tell Matt I love him. He doesn't say anything back.

Jen, speak up. Maybe he didn't hear you! That's it. That's the reason! Can they lower the music inside of this bar, please? Why do they have to play the Chainsmokers so loud that my sinuses are forced to dance too?

It's the first time I've ever said those words to a person—first. So I say them again, this time clearing my throat, pushing what feels like a pack of Legos out of my esophagus. "Hey, I, umm, I just said I love you?"

This time, his eyes collapse and his left palm scoots closer toward the edge of the bench. If a body could speak, his would say, "Excuse me, could you help me locate the nearest exit?"

But I don't care. I shake my neck, wondering if sound is coming out of it.

Our logic takes a nap when we're anxious. It goes for a long pissed-off walk in the opposite direction when we refuse to

2. YOU WILL STILL TRY TO FIND LOVE

accept the obvious. Because if I would have accepted the obvious, I would have understood that silence is the loudest thing a person can say to us if we listen. But in those moments, we're usually not listening.

I stand up from the bar seat and raise my hands in the air. If I'm going to try again, I might as well make sure he and the rest of this Lower East Side dive bar can hear me.

"Listen to me!" I belt out, during the chorus of "Roses." "I think I love . . ."

"You two!" Ry interrupts, comes over, and bear hugs us both. I've known Ry since high school, since the days of passing notes to crushes and getting kissed for the first time. The days of wondering if love was the same feeling as heart burn and if not, if it felt like walking on top of marshmallows.

Even though Ry has known me through braces, a punk rock phase, and the time I almost got my lip pierced, he has apparently never learned to read my face for misery, because when he sees me in that moment he says, "Whoa, Jen. What's come over you? You look like you're on cloud nine!"

"More like cloud call 911," I mumble.

Matt finally speaks, ruling out my grand theory that maybe his lack of a response throughout all of this was because he was unconscious.

"Ha! Another beer, man?" he says to Ry.

Finally the Bride

Ry downs what's left in his cup and he and Matt go to the bar. I lock myself inside a bathroom the size of a coffin, wondering if I've sealed my own death in this unofficial 4-month relationship.

Days later, I hear from Matt:

"You know what you said to me at the party?"

"That I liked green grapes over red?"

"No?"

"That I didn't like Drake's music?"

"No!"

I knew what he was talking about. Love makes you a thousand things, but it doesn't make you stupid. But this time, he deserved to bring it up.

"That thing you said before Ry interrupted us?"

"Yep," I concede.

"Well, I, um, I think I feel the same?"

He loves me! He really loves me! He can't say the words, but he kind of said the words. It counts! I swear it counts.

But it doesn't. If I wasn't in such a DDD, a delusional desperate daze, I would have been sober enough to hear what he really said.

He thinks that he feels the same. Question mark.

If I had shared that with any of you, in the moment, you hopefully would have said the obvious: no he doesn't.

2. YOU WILL STILL TRY TO FIND LOVE

Days later, he calls again. This time, with a change of plans. "Listen, I'm going to move to Thailand for a few months."

"Oh," I feel the swooshing liquid of a breaking heart start to climb up my epiglottis.

"Well, I'll come too! I work from home." I just got laid off. My career as a freelancer is starting to take off from my couch. I can work from anywhere.

"No, Jen," he begins.

Love makes you a thousand things. Okay, fine. Sometimes it does make you stupid.

"You're not invited."

Does one need an invitation to give up their entire life and all they have going for them to move to a new country they've never been to before to chase a man who can barely admit he loves her back?

"When you say not invited, you mean what exactly?"

"Jen, don't worry. Wait for me to come back. You'll be single then I'm sure! You're always single! Ha."

Love makes you a thousand things. Sometimes you refuse to let it make you stupid anymore.

Standing in the middle of Fifth Avenue, I drop my purse on the ground, put the call on speaker, and shake the phone in the afternoon sky.

"NO I WON'T! NO I WON'T! NO I WON'T!"

Finally the Bride

It took fifteen missed calls, twenty texts, five emails, and a handful of Facebook messages for Matt to believe me. It took zero seconds for me to believe it myself. Finally.

I wish I could tell you that was the end of this particular episode, but it was not. Feeling bereft, I did something very stupid: I texted the guy I'd loved before the guy who didn't love me back. Nate.

I was at my lowest.

Look at you, love, making me stupid again. Nate and I had ended things a year before, for good. We'd been parallel lines trying to force ourselves to make it in the world together. We were never meant to intersect. I knew that, but still, I couldn't help but text him: "Nate, it's me. Hey! How are things?"

After a long twenty-seven hours of waiting for a reply, my phone lit up and my heart dimmed to the darkest place yet. "Jen, what we had is over. Locked up and sealed in a place I will never go back to. Leave me alone, okay?"

"Okay," I sang into the empty corridor of a chilly apartment refusing to accept the artificial heat pumping into the air. *Okay, Okay, Okay.*

Chapter 3

SOMETIMES IT DOESN'T HAPPEN

The first wedding I remember going to was at a restaurant overlooking the World Trade Center a year before it collapsed. My dad dragged me to the window in the corner of the room with the best view, the one right behind the chuppah, and tilted me sideways. "Jenny, look!" he said, and there, close by, were two of the biggest towers I had ever seen in my life. They looked like they belonged so high up in the sky, like they were a part of this universe, like they were meant to exist.

I remember wishing I felt the same about myself. But at eleven, with thick braces that could scratch a cheek worse than a cat's claw and a training bra that protected boobs the shape of birthday hats, I didn't feel like I belonged anywhere. Especially at this fancy wedding where the guests looked like they couldn't breathe in their zipped-up, dry-clean-only outfits that were visibly two sizes too small.

Everything I knew about weddings I learned from 90s romcoms featuring Julia Roberts: sometimes there's a nasty love

Finally the Bride

triangle featuring the groom's best friend, and sometimes the bride has second thoughts and leaves the ceremony, before saying I do, on a giant stallion. I was hoping this wedding would prove all of that wrong.

But ten minutes after the ceremony was supposed to start, the rabbi stood in front of a room of peevish guests, tapping his toes and eyeing his Rolex.

"You know," the man next to me started to say, loosening his bow tie and taking out a tissue to blow his nose. "Sometimes these things don't happen."

In the distance, platters of hors d'oeuvres, cheese and crackers, and buffet chafing dishes with closed lids (which I hoped contained my favorite foods—chicken nuggets, mac 'n' cheese, and French fries—because what else would they feed you at a wedding?) sat idle, ready to be served any minute.

"You mean the food?" My stomach giggled nervously.

"No!" He leaned in, sliding his chair closer to mine. "Sometimes the bride doesn't show up!"

"To the party or . . . ?"

I didn't want him to know how naive I was. I was trying to pass for thirteen because people took thirteen-year-olds more seriously than eleven-year-olds. *You're a teen, act like it,* they'd say when I lied about my age, and I liked that because it taught me things other eleven-year-olds didn't know yet,

3. SOMETIMES IT DOESN'T HAPPEN

like you can't eat with your fingers in public, and people will be offended when you roll your eyes at them.

I didn't want this stranger to know I was an amateur wedding guest. That the only way I'd ever celebrated anyone's holy matrimony was through a television screen as I sucked on strings of licorice, in pajamas, on the couch.

"I went to a wedding where the bride never showed up."

"Wait, like Julia Roberts?"

"Huh?" He scrambled. "Kid. She didn't come. She stuck a fork in the relationship. We later found her cashing in their honeymoon plane tickets for a month's stay in Tahiti."

"Whoa." Real life was exactly like those Hollywood blockbusters. *I knew it.*

"I heard she ended up marrying the wedding photographer, John."

"John?"

"Yeah, you would have never guessed it was John."

For a while after that, every time I met someone named John, I gave him the side-eye and wondered if he was the one who had ruined everything.

Finally the Bride

Years later, stuck in traffic in the middle of Times Square, I admit to a coworker that I think I'm dating the wrong person.

"How do you know?" she asks, honking the horn at a stopped car in front of us.

"When he brings up marriage, mortgages, making babies, my skin breaks out in hives in the shape of mini *x*'s."

Stepping on the gas, she wrestles with pockets of air in her throat. I can tell she has an opinion, but she's not certain she wants to let it out.

"I once married the wrong person," she confesses, a one-up brag she clearly doesn't use often.

"Did you know at the wedding?"

"I remember walking down the aisle, looking at crying guests, thinking to myself, this is going to have to suck to do again!"

I sit in the passenger seat with my mouth buckled shut, thinking about how many steps down the aisle it would take me to feel the same way about the guy I am spending my weekends with. My estimate? Three.

"I was texting another guy in the bathroom right before the ceremony started."

Was his name John? I think to myself.

"I didn't want to let people down. I went through with the wedding. I stayed married for a year!"

3. SOMETIMES IT DOESN'T HAPPEN

"Do you feel bad about it?"

"My biggest regret was, not walking down the aisle, throwing my hands up in the air, and saying, 'Sorry people! Sometimes it doesn't happen like you all thought it would!'"

Sometimes it doesn't happen.

I say those words to brides when they hire me to tell them the truth. As their "professional bridesmaid," they ask me things they are embarrassed to ask their friends, like is it okay to have second thoughts, and is cold feet a real thing?

They tell me things too.

Five minutes into my first session with a bride named Cynthia, she gets right to the point:

"Anyone ever call the whole thing off?" She chews on her lip and picks at her cuticles.

It's more than obvious that something is wrong. It's the middle of winter, and she's sweating through her blouse like she just left a sauna.

I nod my head and she deflates, like someone poked her with a needle, letting out stale air that's been keeping her sitting up straight with a tacky smile.

Finally the Bride

"Oh, thank God," she says. "I didn't hire you to be my bridesmaid. I hired you to help me end my wedding."

Sometimes it doesn't happen.

This is the line I repeat in my head, like a trance-induced mantra, as I sting with panic, towering over a bride named Rose, who minutes ago, grabbed me by the wrist, pulled me into a room, and locked the door.

"Jen," she cries out. "I hate the groom."

Sometimes it doesn't happen.

"Okay," I respond, my heart beating so fast it sounds like crickets attacked my voice.

The wedding was supposed to start ten minutes ago, over 150 guests are seated, the bridal party is lined up, and the song people will walk down the aisle to is queued up, with a DJ who won't stop asking when he can press play.

"Did you, um, realize this, uh, right now?"

"That's not how it works, Jen!" she yells back, like I'm some sort of professional. Then I remember that I am. I'm supposed to be good at this wedding chaos thing. But even after working over fifty weddings a year, for years straight, moments like

3. SOMETIMES IT DOESN'T HAPPEN

this completely unravel all of my qualifications. "I guess yes. Maybe no. Who cares? I don't want to get married!"

I think back to the guy in the bow tie, the coworker behind the wheel, to Julia Roberts on the horse. People are going to do what they want to do. You can't always stop them. That's not your job. Perhaps in situations like these, your only job is to help them live out their getaway plan or point them toward the nearest exit.

"You don't have to get married." I wrap my arms around her, blowing out her invisible smoke signals. "I'll call us an Uber. We'll go get pizza."

She moves away from me and sits on the couch. Tossing her head back in her beautiful white dress with pearls along the seams, she exhales what feels like a year's worth of stress.

Then it all hits me, the other side of the story.

I think about the people who are left pacing back and forth on their wedding day, wondering if the person they are supposed to marry is stuck in traffic, went to the wrong venue, rode off on a stallion without sending them the memo. What about their story? What about how it all ends for them?

If I let her sneak out the window, my karma will go to shit. What if I never find the person who will make me eager to sprint down the aisle and marry them? Or worse. I find someone I love dearly only for them to pull a Cynthia on me?

Finally the Bride

Maybe our lives aren't anything like the movies. Maybe the real difference is that we can control who we hurt and how we hurt them.

"But first, you and the groom have to talk."

I step out of the bridal suite and stick the groom inside of it, locking the door and setting a timer on my phone for ten minutes. When the beeping goes off, whatever they decide, I'll help them carry it out, but at least it won't be a surprise.

"Jen, what are you thinking?" Ashley, a bridesmaid, storms down the hall, waving her wilting bouquet in the air. "They have to go through with this!"

"I spent so much money on this wedding!" the mom yells in my face. I can taste her lipstick-stained spit.

"What a shitshow," the best man squeaks, twisting off the cap of a flask and downing the liquid inside with just one gulp.

My eyes roll at each of them, one by one.

Sometimes it doesn't happen.

When the timer goes off, I enter the room.

"So?"

"We aren't in love," Rose says.

I flutter my lips.

"But we're going to go through with it. Fake it for our guests," the groom chimes in.

3. SOMETIMES IT DOESN'T HAPPEN

The DJ plays the song and we walk down the aisle, the bride last, with tears bouncing out of her eyelids.

When it comes time for them to say "I do," it's as if the universe begs them not to.

Right as Rose opens her mouth to read her vows, a summer rainstorm hits down so hard it breaks the white tent we're all underneath, and water gushes in. If this were a movie, the sound effects would drown out the guests' screaming. But in real life, 150 people yell so loudly and scatter in different directions, no one actually hears if Rose says "I do" to spending a life together, *till death do them part*, with the groom.

I stay standing next to Rose, our dresses turning soggy, and watch her eyes and her lips curl upward, as if the rain was her secret backup plan all along.

Hours later, I make my secret exit, skipping goodbyes and hailing a taxi to take me back to my real life, where I'm not hired to pretend to be someone's best friend, or in this case partner in crime, for the day, when all of a sudden, the best man grabs my arm.

"Dude, you saved this wedding!" His hug brings up a sudden feeling of nausea I've been swallowing since this morning.

"Let me tell you something," I say, pushing him away. "Friendship isn't forcing other people to do what you want them to do. Sometimes it doesn't happen. Because it's not supposed to! This is real life and these are real human beings!"

Finally the Bride

"Yeah, but today it did!" He burps up some whiskey, pats me on the butt, and walks back into a flooded wedding party where the currents are drifting the bride and the groom further and further apart.

Days later, I call it off.

"I have cold feet," I tell the guy who gives me hives.

"But we're not getting married We're just dating?"

"Yeah, but one day we will, and I mean this in the best way I can mean it, I just don't want to have heavy feet walking down the aisle."

Minutes later, he is gone. There won't ever be engagement photos of us in the shredder and a completed wedding registry of gifts we'd have to return and guests fighting with airlines about nonrefundable plane tickets they no longer have a use for. Our story ends before anyone else has a chance to get involved.

Years later, I see on Instagram that he's married now, with a kid, and I wonder if he thought about me on his wedding day. If he asked his wife-to-be if she had cold feet. If he told her about a girl who just wasn't sure she'd make it down the aisle or not.

3. SOMETIMES IT DOESN'T HAPPEN

Sometimes it doesn't happen.

But then again, sometimes it does.

Chapter 4

TO FIND ONE, FIRST FIND MANY

"He's staring at you," Dana the bride says, and she's right. The barista behind the counter at Starbucks is eyeballing me as he's pouring a latte, foaming at the mouth.

"No, he's not." I look away from the smooth macchiato of a human and turn my focus on Dana. "Even if he is, it's probably because I have a milk mustache or a coffee stain on my crotch that you're not telling me about."

Dana exhales so loud it sounds like she's growling. I scan the room and let my eyes wander back to the barista. He is indeed staring and it bothers me. I don't know why. It's not like I'm the most beautiful person here. Or at least I just don't feel like it. For starters, I'm wearing gym clothes. Used gym clothes. I met Dana after a spin class that I didn't even wash my hands after, let alone wipe any sweat off my forehead. It must still be there, I think, rubbing my temples, feeling what feels like dried glue on construction paper.

4. TO FIND ONE, FIRST FIND MANY

Ah, that's it! He's not admiring me for my looks. He's playing the good old game of "Is she sweating or did she just take a shower?"

"Jen! Earth to Jen!" Dana yelps.

I shake my head and come back to the reality that is the true reason why I'm here, today, at this very Starbucks: Dana is paying me to be here.

I'm her hired bridesmaid.

Dana has friends, plenty of them, but they all have a story. Some of them threatened to wear blue bridesmaid dresses instead of the lilac color she picked. One of them, the groom's sister, told her there's a 20% chance she'll make it to the wedding because she has a grudge against everyone. Another sister is only sixteen but can drink like she's twenty-one. The kind of help Dana needs can't be asked of a wedding planner. It's the job of one person and one person only—me.

We're here today to strategize about the drama as if we're playing a game of human chess, so I know when I show up at her wedding dressed in a bridesmaid dress, pretending to know her from yoga class, who needs to move diagonally, vertically, or horizontally, but most importantly, who cannot cross paths with one another.

"Wait a second," I pause the talk about her bridal party misfits to ask a question I forgot to ask when we first met. "How'd you meet your fiancé?"

Finally the Bride

At the time, I had worked with close to thirty brides, and my own data showed that over 85% of them met their fiancés on dating sites, followed by meeting through mutual friends, a few through work, and a tiny, itty bitty few through a meet-cute that belonged in a rom-com, like here, at a coffee shop.

Those kind of love stories happen—but they don't happen to me. All my attempts at meeting Mr. Right in person seem to go really, really wrong.

I once flirted with a guy on the subway and decided to miss my stop and keep talking to him, hoping he'd give me his number. I ended up a half hour deeper into Queens than I ever wanted to be, and when he finally went to get off at his stop, and I got the courage to yell, "Wait, don't go yet!" the door slammed between our bodies, and I ended up in an area called Flushing (the furthest part of Queens you can go to by subway) and he went I don't know where, but it didn't matter because our chances of meeting again were a royal flush.

Once at a bar, I made an instant connection schmoozing a guy with whiskey breath that made my body feel like mush. After cheersing and slow dancing in the corner to a Hozier song, he asked for my number. It was only after he left the bar that I realized the number I gave him was wrong. I had given him my home phone number that I memorized in fourth grade that was no longer my family's. It turns out no matter how hard you ugly cry on the phone with AT&T at 4 am,

4. TO FIND ONE, FIRST FIND MANY

they have zero sympathy for situations like this and refuse to disconnect the new person who your old phone number from childhood belongs to now.

"Ready for this?" Dana begins, and I find instant excitement in learning where a sassy but caring, assertive but anxious person like her met her match.

"Let me guess," I say, channeling my inner psychic Diane. "A speed dating event? Plenty of Fish? You seem like a Plenty of Fish kind of girl!"

Dana chugs her coffee and rolls her eyes. That's the thing. When you hire me as a bridesmaid, you get the friend you sometimes wish you never had.

"I turned dating into a game and went on as many first dates as I could on Saturdays and Sundays. Sometimes between four and six a day. I kept track of the guys on an Excel spreadsheet and tracked things like where they went to college, what their hobbies were, their projected income, and scored them based on that."

"What the actual . . ."

"It took me less than a month to meet Dave."

I grab my wrist and check my pulse, eager to see if I'm actually sitting here listening to this or if I passed out and this is all one of those dreams you repeat back later, and the person laughs along with you because they too can't believe how cuckoo you sounded in your slumber.

Finally the Bride

"How did you not just give up? Going on those dates must have made you miserable! I go on one a month, and I need extensive therapy and a break from society for weeks after!"

"No," she shoots back. "You get immune to it. Coffee dates. Forty-five minutes max, and then you leave, walk around the block, reapply lipstick, and do it all again."

I can't tell if Dana is telling the truth or if she is threatening me with what my future will look like if I don't walk up to the barista and ask for his number, but whatever she is doing is working.

"You should try it, Jen, since you're clearly never going to meet anyone in person." Ouch. She shrugs her shoulders and purses her lips. She's the most persuasive person I've ever met because as soon as she finishes her sentence, my chair and this conversation are left behind. I am walking toward the barista.

"Just wanted to say nice job with this latte." I look down at my grandé.

"Yeah, cool," he says back, fast.

I stay there anyway, twisting the green splash stick and squeezing out my best smile.

"Anything else I can help you with?" he asks, looking off in the distance, far away from where I'm standing, back to where I was sitting.

"Yeah, well," I go on, thinking about how if this doesn't work out then I'll have to march back to Dana and ask her

4. TO FIND ONE, FIRST FIND MANY

to make me an Excel spreadsheet for competitive dating. "It's just that my friend, Dana, and I are having a bet. She thinks you're staring at me." I giggle.

"You?" he says as a question.

"Me," I reply as his answer.

I turn around, squint my eyes, and that's when I see it: outside on the street corner are a group of naked women with body paint dancing the Electric Slide. We are in Times Square. How could I think I could be the center of anyone's attention when the view from this coffee shop has better people-watching than any other window in the world?

I want to lie to Dana. I want to tell her that he was indeed looking at me, but after speaking more, we just weren't a good match. He likes things no one else does. Like hockey and doing laundry.

But Dana sees me and instantly knows. It's like rejection is a perfume she's sprayed on too many people before. She smells it on me.

"It's a numbers game," Dana says, packing up her notebook.

Here I am, getting advice from someone who treats dating like you'd treat car shopping, yet I can't stop thinking about her technique. It seems exhausting, a bit much, and quite unlikely to end well, but I do want to see if it is something I can survive.

Finally the Bride

"To find the one, Jen, first you have to find many." Dana leaves me with her wise words and sticks her middle finger up at the barista.

I take the train home, sitting on an empty bench in the subway, re-downloading the dating apps I've deleted many times before: Hinge. Tinder. Coffee Meets Bagel.

What if I just go on four dates a weekend? Two on Sunday and two on Saturday? That's it.

But maybe that's not enough? If I am going to try this, I am going to max out my effort and then never try dating again, believe Psychic Diane, and just adopt a bunch of cats or join a nunnery or get involved in a club for women who just weren't meant to find love.

Across from me on the train are rotting subway ads for Valentine's Day parties from just days before.

"February 14th," I say out loud. "What a horrible day."

February 14th. February 14th. February 14th.

The more I say the date in my head, the more the number fourteen haunts me. It's an evil day for anyone single, and it would be a painful amount of dates for a single woman to go on in one month.

Fourteen dates in one month? Whoa. Why not?

From February 18th until March 18th, I'll date like it's my job. Then, I'll quit. Show the world, Dana, and Diane

4. TO FIND ONE, FIRST FIND MANY

that I tried so hard, and it's just not for me. That there's no one in the dating pool who is meant to be my synchronized swimmer.

Before I log back into the dating apps, I set some rules:

1. You must say yes to every single guy who asks you out on a date.
2. You must ask any guy you're remotely interested in out on a date.
3. No date will be longer than forty-five minutes.
4. If after the first date, you are not excited by the idea of ever seeing them again, you can say no to a second date.
5. No one I go on a date with is to know that he is part of this 14-date challenge.

I sit on my couch and swipe for fifteen minutes, connecting with three guys who swipe yes on me and copying the same message to them.

"Jen here. Skip the small talk and meet for coffee on Saturday?"

One never writes back. Two say yes.

Lesson one learned: it is a waste to go back and forth on these apps chatting about the weather, current events, and how our day is. Most people want the same end goal anyway, to meet in person.

Three more people slide into my DMs and I arrange to meet them for coffee on Sunday. I ask three guys out for

Finally the Bride

a Tuesday night date and two respond, "Sure." One never writes back.

I don't spend more than five seconds on their profiles and can hardly verify that they aren't creepy. But I am not on these apps to over-judge. I am there to fill a spreadsheet with potential suitors.

Here's who I have for round one:

- **Saturday:**

  Joe

  Michael

  Ron

- **Sunday:**

  Lucas

  Scott

On Saturday, I put on my long-lasting lip stain and arrive at the coffee shop early to get a decaf coffee. It is going to be a long day, and I decide to skip the caffeine until the start of date two.

Joe arrives fifteen minutes later, which cuts into my next date time, so as we sit down, I tell him I have family coming in so we'll have to make this quick, which is fine because Joe is the kind of guy that doesn't let anything bother him. You could tell him the world is about to end and he'd be like, "Right on, let's go do dim sum." And I'm the kind of person that if you told them the world is ending, I'd stand on the ta-

4. TO FIND ONE, FIRST FIND MANY

ble, throw the napkins in the air, and run a marathon around the city in sheer panic. So after twenty-five minutes, when Joe's espresso is almost empty, I say it was great to meet him. I am going to use the restroom and then head out. He nods his head, squeezes the cup in his hand, and hugs me goodbye.

I take a deep breath, wash my hands, and wait for Michael.

When Michael arrives, we hug hello, and I order a small hot coffee before jumping into a conversation that for some reason centers around Uber and taxi cars only. When I try to change the topic to learn more about this potential suitor, he goes back to Uber. I don't know why. He doesn't work for Uber, he hardly takes Uber, but he just wants to talk about Uber.

Finally, Ron. I order a tea. Five minutes in he mentions the word *wife*, which isn't him asking me prematurely to marry him, it is him telling me that he has a wife.

"You mean you have a wife right now?" I ask, shocked.

"Yes, kind of."

"There's no kind of. It's yes or no."

"Yes, but."

"There's no but."

"Yes, I want to get divorced soon."

Ron is the final date of the day. I think about dumping the hot tea on his jeans. But I already caused a scene at this coffee shop with Dana days ago, and now I am running my dating

Finally the Bride

ring from it and just don't want to bring more attention from the security guard. So I get up, push my chair in, say the nastiest group of words I can think of in the moment, and go home.

The rest of the fourteen dates go as follows:

Henry—I agree to a dinner date because he mentions pizza. When I get there, he asks me if I know anywhere he can get coke. I say ask the waiter. He says not that kind of coke. I say I no longer feel so hungry and get up and leave.

Brett—I agree to an after work happy hour drink date with a guy who doesn't say a word to me. I spend forty-five minutes wondering if he is shy or just doesn't like me. I mention the patterns of the wallpaper on three different occasions just to fill the silence. That 45-minute date feels like 45 hours.

Greg—Toward the end of the date, Greg starts to cry. He tells me he has to go home next month because his mom sold their childhood home and he needs to give away his stuff. At the time, I can't see why something like that would make a grown-up cry, so I pat him on the back and say I have to get going. Years after that moment, I have to do the same thing, and it is heartbreaking. So, Greg, wherever you are, I feel you, and I'm sorry I never spoke to you again. You were right! Throwing out fifteen years' worth of yearbooks is the kind of moment that makes you feel like a monster.

4. TO FIND ONE, FIRST FIND MANY

Paul is thirty-eight and looking to get married in the next six to nine months. I am looking for a second date, maybe third. I can't meet his fast track.

Roger tells me he spends most of his money on going to music festivals, and I say I like music, and he says he doesn't. He likes watching the girls in no clothing, and I think wow, you're admitting that on a date.

Everett brings up his recent ex, first, and so I tell him about the guy who most recently broke my heart, and by the end of the date we are holding hands crying over lost love.

Frank tries to kiss me, and I nearly punch him in the nose.

Wes tells me he thinks that me being a lifelong vegetarian is a little aggressive, and he is going to get me to eat meat again.

Justin leaves me with a bill of $100, because he goes to the bathroom and never comes back.

Peter actually picks his nose in front of me, examines what comes out of his schnoz, and then flicks it across the room.

Seth finds out I started a business and tells me he wants to be an entrepreneur, so he asks the waiter for a napkin and a pen and pounds me for business advice. After ten minutes of that, I try to change the subject, but he says, "No, this is no longer a date! This is a business development session!"

Finally the Bride

Finally, March 18th comes. I am done. I barely have a voice, can hardly keep the guys straight, am sick of hearing myself give the elevator pitch of what I do for work, and most of all, feel lousy. There wasn't one person whom I connected with. Nobody who made me laugh hard enough, think deep enough, or feel different enough.

I text Dana first.

"Bad advice. Met nobody. That's all I have to say. See you for our session on Thursday."

Then, I go to each app and delete them as quickly as I can.

Goodbye, Tinder. See you never again, JSwipe. Later, Plenty of Fish.

When I go to the final app, Hinge, it won't let me delete it until I clear my profile. As I am deleting my photos and erasing my profile, a message pops up.

"Hey, Jen. Our match is expiring in a few hours. I'm sorry we didn't have a chance to chat. Here's my number if you want to meet for coffee."

You have to be crazy, Jen, I think to myself. *You're so done.*

But right as my fingers go to delete the app and the message, they betray me and copy the number into my phone.

"Adam, it's Jen. From Hinge. If you want to meet me, let's do coffee tomorrow at noon."

What's one more? It is almost like a prize dangling in my face. If I can have fourteen bad dates, fifteen will mean I'll

4. TO FIND ONE, FIRST FIND MANY

feel even better at being self-destructive. At not dating for the next year and taking a solo trip to the moon.

I keep repeating that in my head as I go to the coffee shop and sit in a chair, like I have done fourteen times before that month, and wait for someone to come in, hardly recognize me, and chat in circles about nothing too memorable, until the date expires and we go our sad separate ways.

Nah, I don't want to do this. I stick my arms in my tomato colored coat, unbend my knees. *I don't need to do this.* Date number fifteen is just not something I want to stick around for.

But as I go to grab my purse, the door swings open, and in walks a guy with Disney eyes and curly, gelled hair, arms wide open, mouth agape.

"Jen!" he says, loud with punctuation, and in that moment, everyone in the coffee shop turns their head to look at this person with me.

There he is. Date number fifteen. A guy named Adam Kossoff. A guy with big hair and an even bigger personality. And I have no idea when he walks into the coffee shop that he will eventually be the one to put an end to all of this. That exactly three years and four months later, he'll trick me into going for a walk on the beach so he can ask me to marry him. But all I know in that moment is that my coffee tastes a little bit different, and I feel a little bit different too.

Finally the Bride

Dana, I think when Adam makes me out of breath from laughing for the third time that coffee date, *You were right. You were so right.*

P.S. Dana, this chapter is for you. Without your experiment challenge dating extravaganza, I don't know if I would have ever met Adam. And it makes me happy every single day that I did. I owe you a coffee. Shoot, I owe you the entire coffee shop!

Chapter 5

HOW TO MESS UP A RELATIONSHIP

*I did not just fall in love.
I made a parachute jump.*
-Zora Neale Hurston

The first time Adam tells me he loves me, I tell him he's wrong.

"You don't even know me!" I toss back, angry that he'd confess something so serious to someone he seriously didn't know. We'd been dating for only two months, seeing each other once or twice a week.

"How could you love a person you've only seen a dozen or so times in your life?"

What he didn't know was that the first time I told someone I loved them (that wasn't related to me) was in middle school, after spending weeks chatting back and forth with BaseballGuy078. We met in an AOL chat room. He said his name was Ryan. He said he lived in Washington. He believed me when I said I was a model. I cut a photo of Mandy Moore out of *Seventeen* magazine and scanned it over as proof I was a real woman.

"You're beautiful," he typed back.

"I think I love you," I responded.

I was thirteen and didn't know a thing about love, but I acted like I did. I was an expert at breaking my own heart.

In middle school, the boys made fun of me for doing the opposite of what the other girls were doing. For wearing sports bras over padded ones from Victoria's Secret, for gelling my hair back into tight ponytails instead of squeezing a hot iron over my almond-brown strands, for being on the softball team and not the cheerleading squad, for showing off my acne when I could have hidden the red dots with expensive makeup from one of those beauty counters at the mall.

"You'd be a lot better looking if you didn't look like you," Brian told me after a group of boys ran by and laughed.

I turned bright red, wondering how middle school boys got so good at acting like they were judges at some beauty pageant.

"Maybe do something. I don't know," he screamed out as I stood still, as statuesque as possible. "Do something like the other girls do."

I was in love with Brian. He was the first boy to talk to me one-on-one all year. Maybe he was trying to tell me he loved me by telling me to change. So I did. I brushed my hair and

5. HOW TO MESS UP A RELATIONSHIP

borrowed my mom's flat iron. I put on a bra I stole from a classmate during a sleepover. I put tinted cream all over my face and my pimples looked skin-colored. I wrote Brian a note:

"Hiii, so, thanks for talking to me. Want 2 hang out at Jessica's party on saturday? I'll be there 'cuz softball practice is canceled. U?"

I dropped it in his hand during science class. Everyone around him giggled. He moved the paper around in his fingers, dropped it in the trash, and later told me never to go up to him in public again.

I realized love was less about changing who you are for people and more about changing who you love.

Which is why when Adam tells me he loves me, I fight to make sure he's not making that same mistake.

"If you tell someone you love them too soon, you'll get hurt too fast."

Here I am, morphing from rookie girlfriend to truth-sayer.

Adam makes waves with his eyes. I don't think he's ever gotten himself tangled with someone who speaks like they are constantly brainstorming copy for a self-help book.

But he doesn't sulk in what I say, doesn't even let those sentences enter his ears. He's ready with the defense.

Finally the Bride

"Jen, you're wrong," Adam says, as if one is ever right when it comes to being the first to confess new love. "You're unlike anyone I've ever met, and we have a special connection."

"NO! NO! NO!" I shout back. It's nighttime and we're in my tiny Manhattan apartment. I want to leave, but I have no other place to go. I want to tell Adam to leave, but I don't know if that's what I really want. I just want him to understand.

"You don't know me!" I yell. "When you get to know me, you won't love me anymore!"

I think about all the guys I've loved before and what they said when it all fell apart:

You're not the person I fell in love with.
I don't think I love you anymore.
You're too much for one person to love.
I thought I loved you, but, Jen, I love the idea *of you.*

And I think about Adam and what he'll say to me when he realizes I was, indeed, right.

A month later, I get a phone call from my mom.

When I answer, there's silence. I know she's on the other end of the phone because I hear her breathing. I hear her making the sounds of someone opening their mouth and

5. HOW TO MESS UP A RELATIONSHIP

pushing out words, except the words sound like throat gargles. It's the sound of someone lighty coughing up sand.

"What's wrong? What happened?"

My mom starts to speak, and I don't know when or how it happens, but my body slides down onto the ground of Fifth Avenue. Suddenly, I go silent. What she tells me makes my insides weak. I claw the pavement. I drop my phone.

That 15-minute conversation pokes giant holes in my life. Everything changes. The news is so difficult to understand, hear, and accept that I don't have the energy to get up off the ground for what feels like an hour, and even then, I wobble home like I've just finished running a marathon.

You don't need to know what she said or what happened, but you do need to know it involved someone I love dearly. Someone I love dearly was sick and in trouble. We had entered the middle of this person's story, where the problem played out and there was no clear ending. It was the kind of situation where the ending would be unknown for years.

In every person's life, they'll have a moment where they find something out that changes everything. In that moment you won't know what to do, so you will do a lot of nothing.

I stare at the living room wall in my apartment for two hours and seventeen minutes. Then I finally call the guy who told me he loved me just a few weeks ago.

Finally the Bride

"Something happened," I say, feeling that familiar struggle to get the words out.

He is at work but offers to leave. He can sense it is an emergency and asks if he should call for help.

"I'm okay," I say. "No, I'm not okay."

When he gets to my apartment, I tell him everything.

"My life is about to get really bad, really hard, and for a really long time," I tell him. Our last three months roll out in my head like a photo album that's hardly filled up.

I sit there and wonder if this is the news that will prove I was right all along. That his "I love you" was just too premature, decided on a dozen or so moments of adventurous dates around New York City with a woman who seemed so donut-eyed about life. For him to realize he loved the idea of who I was before my life was put inside a washing machine and completely shaken up. Now that he's heard what he has heard, will he snap out of this googly-eyed state of infatuation for me and pack up and go?

Adam's head is down, he's breathing harder, he probably regrets falling in love with me, wonders if he can buy something on the internet to erase those feelings.

"Look. Listen," I say. "Things will get really bad soon, and maybe you should leave now. There's the door. If you leave, I won't judge you. I won't add you to the list of people who

5. HOW TO MESS UP A RELATIONSHIP

broke my heart. Honestly, I'd understand. I'd probably consider doing the same."

Adam sits there, stone cold and stiff. I inch closer to a decorative throw pillow that has no purpose on the couch other than to be squeezed by people in moments when they can't handle all of their emotions alone.

I can't handle waiting for what he is going to do.

I get up and open the door, hoping he'll follow.

A year and two months into dating, I tell Adam I don't know if I can do *this* anymore.

Our leases will be up on the same day in August and it is June. We have begun discussing plans, next steps. Adam is saying things about moving in together, and I am hearing things about marriage, babies, mortgages, and the slow walk further away from the fast-paced career that I want more than anything else.

"I don't know. Oh wow," I start to say. "I just don't know if I can do all of this."

We stand still, together, underneath the buzzing of flies and the city summer temperature that's sticking to our skin.

Finally the Bride

"I don't know if I can be this person, do these things. I don't know if this is for me."

"Listen, we've been through a lot," Adam tries to say. "I know . . ."

"Just stop," I cut him off. "Can we just stop talking about all of this?"

Two months later, we're sitting in the back seat of an Uber, suitcases packed in the trunk, the passenger seat, in between our legs. We gave up our apartments, sold most of our belongings, and decided to spend the next few years living in new cities or apartments every few months. We're on our way to our first city, Portland, but it's on the way back, when we settle into a 1-month rental in Bed-Stuy, Brooklyn, that Adam breaks up with me for the first time.

"I don't think I can do this," he tells me. "I don't think I can do this anymore."

I exhale relief and inhale anger. I knew it would come to an end from the second he told me he loved me before he knew me. *I knew it.*

"We're off track," he explains as I toss a book to the wall. "We've completely lost our way."

5. HOW TO MESS UP A RELATIONSHIP

And I know he's right. We've been dealing with the twists of my traumatic personal *event* that's still going on from the year before. We've been fighting about the stress of having no normalcy, no consistency, no structure to our lives since we started living out of a suitcase and inside other people's homes.

Our relationship is becoming the pattern that slime makes when you throw it up against a wall, as it slides down, holding on to the paint for dear life but spreading in all different directions.

Then there is the time I say, "Maybe we should break up," in a Venice Beach coffee shop that's a block from the beach.

Then there is the time Adam says, "Yeah, I do think you should leave," on Christmas Eve, at his family's house, after an hour fight about who the heck remembers.

Who can forget the time, 32,756 feet above ground, on an airplane ride back east, where I tell Adam he needs to decide soon if he and I are going to carry on *forever,* get married, speak the words that I am the "one."

Also, there is the time Adam tells me, "I don't want to go on like this. It's not working," in a tiny railroad apartment that smells like expired Pine-Sol and lemon-scented Glade PlugIns.

Of course there is the afternoon, after a fight I started about who the heck remembers, where I think it will be a good idea to search for apartments, write a new dating profile, find a good therapist, in case it all comes true.

Relationships fall apart. All the best ones do. You just don't hear it as the talk of the town. There aren't social media posts that say, "HEY! We almost broke up this weekend. It was a real doozy. Adam told me he wasn't sure this was working, and I threw a book at the wall. But we decided to make a game plan to get our relationship working again, and it might not work, but it also might work. Stay tuned!"

No. All you see are two people smiling, with a caption that says, "Perfect love will find you," and you simply wonder why it seems it hasn't.

All relationships go up and go down like the rhythm of our breath. Sometimes the relationship doesn't take such an extreme nosedive until one person's world enters a carnival ride that shakes things up fast.

5. HOW TO MESS UP A RELATIONSHIP

I'd be lying if I said I knew Adam and I would make it. I never knew that.

But I'll tell you this, and it has been something I can't seem to get out of my head. When I pointed to the door and told Adam to leave, he didn't get up. He said *no*. He moved his head left and right. He didn't get off that couch.

And he could have gone, most people would have, but he didn't, and you don't stay if you *think* you love a person, you stay if you *know* you love a person.

So yeah, we've had our moments, and yeah, we almost broke up here and there, but one of us has always stayed when the other opened up that door.

You know what's so odd? Whenever I look at a door and then I look at Adam, I always laugh a little bit.

He'll ask me: "Why are you laughing, Jen? What's funny?"

And I've never had the courage to say that I remember the night when I got up and opened the door, making signals with my hand to help ease him into the decision to leave, how he sat still and eventually I got tired. I closed the door when I realized I couldn't force him to go, I couldn't ruin the relationship before the chance that a million other things could ruin it for us.

I think about how he didn't end up breaking my heart and how neither did I.

Chapter 6

IT'S BEEN AN ADVENTURE GETTING HERE

PART ONE

On Friday afternoon, I paused everything to take a nap. There I was, floating deep into my REM cycle, when Adam Kossoff walked into the room and said, "Wake up! Let's go somewhere!" My eyes wiggled and my mouth opened for a disappointed yawn. I screamed back: "Leave me alone! I don't care where you go, just don't come back here and interrupt my nap." I closed my eyes and twisted back into a dream about driving on a highway in the clouds with a zebra in the backseat. What felt like minutes later, but was actually forty-five minutes later, he was back. "Jenny, come on, get up." This time, I pretended not to hear. "Okay, fine," he said nonchalantly, turning his back. "I'm going for a walk." When you know someone, really know the cute and disgusting things about them, you know what you do to get their blood boiling and their shoelaces tied. If you know me, you know it's the feeling of being left behind, missing out on an

6. IT'S BEEN AN ADVENTURE GETTING HERE

adventure, even one as mundane as going for a walk around the cul-de-sac - that's enough to get me tapping my toes. "I'm up," I texted him, peering out the blinds. Quickly, he came back, told me he wanted to get out of the house, asked to go to Starbucks, then the beach for a walk. "It's so hot." "Please, I want to go to the building my grandparents used to live in." "Ugh fine," I said, invisibly kicking and screaming until I buckled myself in the front seat and we drove. As we started walking onto the beach, I felt the midsummer afternoon stale air turn from muggy to courageous. I felt the saltwater breeze flick my nose. "Yeah, it's beautiful here," I thought, or I said, I'm too stubborn to remember. As we stepped onto the sand, to my right was an adorable blanket, with a sign. It looked like someone was about to get engaged. I thought, *Wow, how nice for that couple*. Adam slowed his pace. He wrapped around me like a knitted wool sweater. He led me toward the blanket. "What, wait, really, me, this, oh my god." "It's been an adventure getting here," Adam started. "It will be forever an adventure with you. Will you marry me?"

PART TWO

They say that your whole life flashes before your eyes right before you die. When you get engaged, a major chunk of it pumps out with every beat of your racing heart, a memory reel of the moments that pushed and pulled you to where you are right now. In front of a person, on one knee, asking you the question you thought, maybe, no one ever would. Later, I asked Adam to recall what he said when he proposed. "Tell me again," I demanded. "Tell me again!" "I said it was an adventure getting here, Jen." "Here as in the beach? Or here as in . . ." He grabbed my hand before I could finish. Before I, Jennifer Sara Glantz, the most outrageously determined, blissfully chaotic, confusingly optimistic, vocally over-the-top human, could say too much. So I thought this: *Look at that, Jen! Someone wants to spend the rest of their life with you . . . you . . . the real version of you. Did you see that coming?* And the answer was no but yes, yes but no, yes because I always knew if I stayed true to who I was, the right person would be along for this adventure, this amazing race. I was right. That person? Well, he came along when I least expected it and stayed, every day, even after I woke up from countless daydreams, and stayed, making me feel like yes, uh-huh, we really are dancing on those clouds.

PART THREE

After going on fourteen first dates in one month, I decided to give person number fifteen a try, before officially swearing off dating for the rest of my life, and that's when Adam walked through the door at Irving Farm Coffee shop in Manhattan. I sat there, covering my shaking with nerves body in a fuzzy

6. IT'S BEEN AN ADVENTURE GETTING HERE

apple red coat as he walked over to me, arms wide like he was giving the air a chest bump and a smile that stretched so long I could see the back of his molars, and he said, "JEN GLANTZ!" in an all-caps-like voice with imaginary exclamation points popping out of his ears. And never in my entire life had a stranger been more excited to see me. At some point, in the middle of our date, we talked about the show *The Amazing Race* and how we both wanted to go on it. When the date ended, we hugged goodbye, he mentioned getting pizza soon, and I saved his phone number in my phone as Adam Amazing Race. And three years and a handful of months later, he's still in my phone as that, and yes, the truth is, we did try out for the show, and we made it to the final round, but what's been the most amazing race of them all is that two complete strangers formed this unbreakable relationship.

Three months into our relationship, my life went through a kaleidoscope of chaos, and I sat Adam down on the couch and pointed to the door and said, "Look. listen. Things will get really bad soon and maybe you should leave now." And I'll never forget that he sat there, stone cold and stiff, and said no.

Do you ever watch *The Amazing Race* and see the couples who win it all? They never win because they are the strongest, or the smartest, or the luckiest. It's because they have

Finally the Bride

something nobody else has. And that thing is that they fight, they fight so hard, they find a way to grab on to each other and dance through it all, feet stepping on one another, even when the music notes are funky, high pitched, mismatched.

The most amazing race you can go on in life is one beside someone who makes your heart swell with courage and melt like Silly Putty. I'll never stop feeling a gobbledygook of things when I think about you plus me and this life.

My dear, Adam Kossoff, this amazing race we're on has us winning it all.

Chapter 7

CONVERSATIONS YOU HAVE WHEN YOU GET ENGAGED

Minutes after getting engaged, I sit on a toilet in a restaurant crying.

Did that really just happen? I can't believe it did.

The toilets around me flush one after another, and I use the loud swirly sound as a chance to let out how I really feel.

AHHHHHHHHHHHHH!

"Is everything okay in there?" someone asks.

"I'm just . . ." I try to think of an excuse, but my mind is busy. "I just need a second."

I flush my toilet and lock eyes with the concerned woman at the sink. She passes me the soap, and I start talking.

"I just got engaged and I . . ."

"Your ring is beautiful! Congrats! You should really think about getting married in the winter. Those weddings are the best! It's so humid in Florida otherwise, and your guests will melt during cocktail hour. You don't want that to happen!"

Finally the Bride

I droop my head down, splash water on my eyes, and walk out without saying goodbye. I must look like a zombie bride. That's fine. To the world, I imagine, soon I'll look like a bridezilla.

Here's something nobody tells you about getting engaged: the excitement only lasts a few seconds. It's like when you buy one of those party poppers filled with confetti, and your stomach rattles with excitement as you count down THREE! TWO! ONE! and finally push out hundreds of brightly colored tiny pieces of paper all over the floor. You had the moment, it felt good, it looked good in pictures, but now you have to figure out a way to clean up the mess.

I waited years for Adam to propose, and when he finally did, I felt my entire body tingle with joy as he got on one knee and asked to spend this lifetime together. It felt extraordinary. It felt right.

I hugged him before I even remembered to look at the ring, and with his arms wrapped around my body, I closed my eyes and tried so hard to make that moment last longer because it was one of the absolute best moments of my life.

7. CONVERSATIONS YOU HAVE WHEN YOU GET ENGAGED

But then the questions start coming at me, and I don't have the answers.

When do you think the wedding will be? Will you have a band? You should have a band! What kind of dress will you wear? Aunt Cynthia wants to do your hair, okay? Maybe you should just elope? Don't you dare elope! Ever think about Botox? You know you have to stop eating pizza and start dieting? You have to invite your second cousin, twice removed. Don't worry, I just texted him an invite. That's okay, right? I know this woman whose daughter hired a photographer, and she was awful. You won't hire her, okay?

My head is spinning. I want to spend a few months *just* being engaged without thinking about any wedding plans. But what nobody tells you is that if you don't have your entire wedding planned out before the proposal, you'll feel like you're entering a boxing ring without the gloves.

I spend the weekend listening to friends and family, nodding my head, plastering on a smile that is all teeth, and pretending to write down their suggestions but writing down question marks instead. I stare down blank Excel sheets. I have been engaged for two days and already feel months behind.

Come on, Jen, I think to myself. *You've been to hundreds of weddings, and hundreds of brides have your number on speed*

Finally the Bride

dial. How can you not pull together what you want for your big day in a matter of hours? What is wrong with you?

Three days after getting engaged, I sit Adam down and hand him the computer.

"WE NEED TO PLAN THIS WEDDING RIGHT NOW!"

His eyebrows stretch up to his hairline.

"We just got engaged though? What's the rush?"

"ARE YOU KIDDING? WHAT'S THE RUSH?"

I pace around in circles. Chatter about being so behind, needing answers to questions, feeling the pressure to plan some big beautiful wedding as if the world cares about me, the infamous professional bridesmaid, like they do a Kardashian. I tell him I can't sleep, I can't eat, I can hardly go to the bathroom without someone telling me I need to match the flowers to the tablecloths!

"You're sort of turning into a bridezilla."

I fall silent. We live in a small Brooklyn apartment. It is practically one room. There aren't doors to slam, but if there were, I would slam them all in this moment.

7. CONVERSATIONS YOU HAVE WHEN YOU GET ENGAGED

Instead, I let out an Ahhhhhhh! and walk outside, forgetting to put on shoes. I have my engagement ring on but no freaking shoes.

People who hardly know you like to ask you the most personal questions.

A cashier at CVS rings me up for the milk, grabs my hand, admires my ring, and asks how much it cost.

A friend of a friend of a friend congratulates me on my Instagram post and sends a message asking how long I'll wait until I get pregnant.

A lady sitting next to me at the nail salon strikes up a conversation after seeing the ring and doesn't ask much about the wedding or if I want bridesmaids. Instead, she parachutes right into a conversation about what my bridesmaids should wear.

"Flower crowns."

"Flower crowns?" I repeat back, twisting my ring around so nobody else will see it and talk to me.

"Yes! I saw them at a store in the West Village, and it would be so nice if your bridesmaids wore flower crowns!"

Finally the Bride

This woman has never been married before. She tells me she never wanted to and the idea of a wedding makes her skin crawl. But for some reason, she won't stop talking to me about flower crowns.

Later, the lady doing my nails asks if that woman was my neighbor, an aunt, someone I see often.

"A stranger," I reply, scratching my head over why she was so stubborn about those flower crowns.

Adam and I finally try to talk about our wedding. We sit on a park bench and start from the top.

"Florida, July, pizza, and live music," I read off our must-have wedding list that took us weeks to agree on.

"Oh! Maybe we do it at a music venue?" he adds in.

"But if we invite everyone to Florida, shouldn't we do this outside by the beach?"

"Excuse me," the woman next to us, who I didn't even see sit down, says. "Sorry to butt in, but I heard you talking about your wedding."

I stare at her, wondering if the universe planted her there as some strange joke. Adam and I took a break from talking about our wedding until just now, just these few seconds,

7. CONVERSATIONS YOU HAVE WHEN YOU GET ENGAGED

and we can't even get a minute in without someone wanting to tell us something about a wedding we're already struggling to plan.

"I don't think you should have a wedding." She shifts around to look us in the eyes. "Just elope! Use the money on a big honeymoon. Fiji! Hawaii! Europe?"

"Okay," I exhale and lean into the advice. Whether or not you hire someone to help you plan your wedding, the strangers of the universe will show up and plan it for you. When they do, you sometimes just have to listen. "Why do you think we should just elope?"

"Because the truth is, nobody really wants to go to a wedding anyway. You think they want to schlepp down to Florida in July for the wedding? No."

We give up on deciding anything. We delight in the stranger's honesty and laugh about it over a cup of coffee that drips onto the short list of wedding plans we later toss in the trash.

Later, I go get my teeth cleaned, and the dental hygienist, while plucking gunk from my gums, asks what my plans are for the wedding.

"Cccccidon'tggggknow," I try to say as the metal tools clank around my mouth.

"I think you should elope. Really I do."

"Mmmmm," I utter out of my throat.

"It's what I did twenty years ago, and it was the best."

Finally the Bride

I shut my eyes.

"We went to Italy, I bought a dress for fifty dollars, and we got married in a hotel lobby with strangers: just the two of us with a bunch of strangers."

I relax inside this conversation. I don't have a choice. If I squirm too much, things will get bloody. I sit still and start to realize that when people want to talk to you about your wedding, they are really just hoping to talk about theirs instead. They want you to listen to their horror stories, their trip down the aisle, the one time they were a guest and the wedding ran out of food, *those kinds of things*. It's not because they don't care about you, even the dearest of strangers do care about you, it's just this is their way of finally telling you the truth about getting engaged.

You can try to plan your own wedding, but it'll never come out the way you wanted it to.

About two months into being engaged, I sit Adam down, again, and hand him the computer.

"Please don't yell," he says, remembering the last time I did this and told him, after only three days of being engaged, that we were too far behind in wedding planning.

7. CONVERSATIONS YOU HAVE WHEN YOU GET ENGAGED

"No, no," I start. "I want to show you what I've been working on."

He rests his head in his hands, curious but not concerned.

Every time someone gave me wedding planning advice, I wrote it down in the form of a decision we'd have to make. I had this long list of things we had to pick and choose, and that's when I realized how little I cared and how much other people cared.

"Listen, I know I love you. I know I want to spend our lives together going on adventures that hardly make sense to anyone else. But when it comes to a wedding, I just don't care what color the napkins are! Heck, they can be paper napkins. I don't care if we have a band or a DJ! I don't care. I never did. You don't either!"

He nods his head and begins looking concerned.

"Did you take our wedding budget and invest it in something funky?"

"Even better," I say. "I did this."

I show him the Finally the Bride website. I built this, secretly, over the last month based on all those wedding decisions everyone told us we had to make. Except, I turned them into polls.

"Why not let strangers vote on our entire wedding? What they pick, we do."

"This is bizarre," Adam responds.

"Wedding planning is bizarre!"

"Jen, you don't listen to anyone. You're really going to listen to a bunch of strangers?"

"Do I have a choice? They are coming at me from all directions with their opinions. At least this organizes things."

Adam asks to think it over, but I start printing business cards with the website on it. Next time someone has something to say about the wedding, I'll hand them a card, and they'll tell me on the website. Our very own wedding-planning suggestion box in the form of online voting.

Adam agrees to do this, and I press publish on the website, kick my feet back, and, for the first time since getting engaged, let air out from my mouth as if I have just finished a hot yoga class.

Here's what nobody tells you about getting engaged: behind every ring proposal picture with the hashtag #ISaidYes is a couple juggling hundreds of expensive decisions and opinions and who have no idea what the heck to do, even if they thought they did before getting engaged.

What nobody tells you is that nothing makes sense before your wedding, but the second it's over, you have a list of mistakes (and bills to pay) that you wish you didn't. That's why everyone wants to shower you with advice.

7. CONVERSATIONS YOU HAVE WHEN YOU GET ENGAGED

You don't have to take it, though sometimes you'll want to, especially when the feedback comes from someone you'll listen to, or in our case, complete strangers who are voting on our wedding plans as if they get a do-over, as if they could yell through the screen, "Don't make so many mistakes!"

How could we when the world is making the decisions for us?

It might sound crazy to you, but if you've been engaged before, you probably felt a little like people were trying to boss your wedding around too, even if you didn't ask them to get involved in the first place, even if you don't even know them. How strange is that?

Chapter 8
IN DEFENSE OF BRIDEZILLAS

"What kind of bride will you be, Jen?"

The first time my friends asked me that question, I was twenty-three years old, and I'd just finished a horrible second date with a guy who picked his nose and used that same finger to dip a chip into our shared bowl of guacamole.

Who cared what kind of bride I'd be when the guys who swarmed my love life were full of crusty boogers?

But before I could answer that question with an eye roll, my friend Jenna, three spicy margaritas deep, answered on my behalf: "Honestly, Jen, you'll probably be the ultimate bridezilla."

The whole table of friends, who had known me since freshman year of college, broke out into a singsong of laughter.

"Why do you automatically think that?" I shot back.

"Because you're already a 'zilla of a person in real life."

Jenna found herself under a spotlight of attention as she painfully retold the stories I had crumpled up and hidden in the back of my mind.

8. IN DEFENSE OF BRIDEZILLAS

I crossed my arms and surrendered to the stories.

The time I lost my purse at a dimly lit nightclub and took it upon myself to find the light switches, turn them all on, and yell and scream until someone found it. The time I gave the silent treatment to almost everyone at the table because I thought they were leaving me out of weekend plans but really they were planning my surprise party.

"Okay, fine," I interrupted Jenna before she could go on to the stories that would really make me squirm. "Maybe you're right. But so what? Is being a bridezilla that bad?"

Everyone lifted their glasses, some filled to the top and others just piles of ice cubes.

"To hoping we're old enough, wise enough, and chill enough to be a bridesmaid for Jen when she FINALLY gets married!"

"Cheers!"

"Is it too bridezilla to ask all of you to buy hair extensions and get a spray tan two days before the wedding?" Jenna asks over group text just a few hours after getting engaged.

Most people respond, telling her they are up for anything she wants.

Finally the Bride

I don't write anything back.

The day before Jenna's wedding, two of her six bridesmaids are no longer speaking to her and are refusing to come to the wedding. Another two got so drunk they are too hungover to come to the ceremony rehearsal. One more decided to add blue streaks to her hair against Jenna's fine-tuned beauty rules.

Then there's me. I've done exactly what Jenna asked. I bought the hair extensions, and I used her woman at the tanning salon to spray my skin orange. I got the $350 dress, the $125 shoes, the $65 purse to match, and I'm carrying an envelope with $300 cash to pay for my hair and makeup for her wedding day.

But none of that matters because when Jenna sees me, she pulls out my hair.

"Jen! Your hair looks so bad. Your extensions look cheap. Take them out. Now!"

I do what she asks.

"And your spray tan! Seriously, you're orange!"

"I thought that was the look you were going for."

"Are you kidding me?" she screams so loud the mirror on the wall of our hotel room shivers. I'm certain the front desk will receive a noise complaint.

"You are literally ruining my wedding right now!"

8. IN DEFENSE OF BRIDEZILLAS

"I want to hire you for my daughter," the voice on the other end of the call says. "She's become a major bridezilla, and I need backup. That's why I called you. That's honestly why I need you."

I have been working as a professional bridesmaid for less than a year. I am too new into the business to say no to new clients, or at least that's what I think. I say yes, unsure of what I am getting myself into and confused as to why people think the word *bridezilla* is so one-size-fits-all.

Fifteen minutes into my first meeting with the bride and her mother, the manager of the Starbucks we're in comes over to kick us out.

"Excuse me, but if you don't stop yelling, I'm going to have to ask all of you to leave. Frankly, well, you're scaring customers."

"We'll settle down, Andy," I say, trying to shush him away so I can jump back into the boxing ring and referee the conversation between the bride and her mom.

They are verbally fist fighting over everything. The bride sent out wedding invitations, and her mom, without telling the bride, designed invitations and sent those out too. The

Finally the Bride

mom wants to wear a white dress that matches the one the bride picked out. The bride doesn't want to invite more than 100 people, and the mom's list of friends and family is already 120. The bride wants to get married in a modern-looking penthouse on the East River. The mom wants her to get married at The Plaza hotel.

I just want this meeting to end and my picture not to be hanging on a wall in the back room of this Starbucks with a circle and an X over it. I want to come back here for an iced almond milk latte with a pump of vanilla whenever the heck I want.

Later, I ask the mom what she thinks the word *bridezilla* really means. Her answer?

"A bride who just can't go with the flow and do what her mom knows is best! "

"Maybe if you stopped being a bridezilla, our wedding day wouldn't be ruined," a groom says to the bride I'm working with minutes before they are supposed to walk down the aisle, exchange their vows, and kiss hello a lifetime together.

The bride starts crying so hard she uses her bouquet to catch the mascara-stained tears.

8. IN DEFENSE OF BRIDEZILLAS

"Hey, Jake!" I step in between them. "Can you grab me your hotel room key? I want to make sure it's all cleaned up after the party ends."

Jake heads to another room to find his wallet and get me a key I don't really need. What I do need is for him to get out of here for a few minutes so I can be alone with the bride.

"Today is a bit stressful, huh?" I ask her in the bathroom, using toilet paper to pat down the water on her face and keep her makeup from sliding down her chin.

"It's just that everyone is calling me a bridezilla, but I'm not! I know I'm not. I'm just trying to make sure today is perfect."

"But no day is perfect," I respond transparently. Why lie to a crying bride? It might seem like the best option. It might seem like the only way to get through the wedding without the drama swelling, but it's not.

It's like going bungee jumping. When you're finally at the top, all your emotions hit, even the misfit ones you've been working overtime to ignore. It all shows up, and right before you jump, you ask yourself a bunch of questions that you need clear answers to.

Should I do this?
Am I making the right choice?
Is it normal to be this nervous?

But when the answers aren't so obvious, so immediate, that's when you desperately need that person in your life to say, "Wait a second, take a step back. Here! Have some water. Let's shake this plan up a bit and see what you really want to do."

Weddings are exactly the same.

"Well it should be! Especially if you're paying $50,000 for it to be," the bride responds. It's obvious what her answers are to those questions. She wants to get married, but she's nervous because she can't afford the party she's about to dance into. That right there is worthy of a breakdown—or sixteen.

This bride isn't a bridezilla. She is a paying customer to the wedding industry, and she wants what she deserves. But what she gets is a missing DJ and a florist who brings wilted bouquets from a wedding the night before. She has the right to cry and scream, demand a refund, and write a nasty Yelp review on the spot. But, instead, those around her are muttering the term *bridezilla* as if the term sums up anyone getting married who shows any sign of emotion other than the Disney-like smile they are expected to have.

That night I Google what *bridezilla* means. It's in the dictionary, you know?

"A woman whose behavior in planning her wedding is regarded as obsessive or intolerably demanding."

But how do you expect someone to act when they are planning a party for every single person they adore in this world,

8. IN DEFENSE OF BRIDEZILLAS

and the party costs them more than anything else they've ever purchased?

How can they stay calm and collected when weddings highlight the weird and the worst in a person's life? Do you know that not every single person has a family dynamic where the people should be in the same room ever? Did you know that not everyone's Thanksgiving dinners contain people sitting down at a table for more than five minutes without an argument taking over? Did you know that some people even get married when they are only 43% sure the relationship will work out?

So we toss brides who act out, like bridezillas, in a bucket and expect them to float on their own.

Or we defend them.

On every live TV interview I've ever done, the host always asks me if I've ever worked with a bridezilla before.

What they are really asking is for me to flip open the book of stories and share the outtakes of a wedding that was so different from the norm; they want the chaotic and shocking.

I have those stories, but I also have positive ones too. Nobody ever asks about those.

Finally the Bride

The question always reminds me of Jenna and how she was so quick to share the moments that made me look like a monster. Those stories never defined me; they were just moments; they passed by and changed. So did I.

"What about grooms?" I usually clap back and ask. "Ever seen a groom fall apart at a wedding? I sure have. I've seen it a lot."

Months after getting engaged, a text message from an unfamiliar number pops up on my phone.

"Hey, Jen! It's Jenna. New phone number LOL." It had been six years since the last day we ever spoke, which happened to be her wedding day. "Congrats on getting engaged! Been a bridezilla yet?"

I spend days wondering if I should respond. A person like that only texts you when they want to feel a certain way about themselves. They want you to text back something that makes them continue on with their lives, thinking everything is under control, thinking they still know you like they think they know you.

I think about my wedding journey so far. The twists and uncertainty, the anxiety around family dynamics, the yells

8. IN DEFENSE OF BRIDEZILLAS

and screams over paying a lot of money for a party that lasts such a small amount of time. The mini fights with Adam over what to do and why we're even doing this wedding thing. The loud sounds that I've belted out over this wedding. The hysterical afternoons and the temper tantrums after reading vendor emails. How the whole thing has felt less like a fairy tale and more like I'm running a small business—managing Excel spreadsheets and people I hired who just never get back to me—and how this is all more than I ever signed up for.

Finally, I take a deep breath and exhale my answer, before blocking her new number, just like I did with the old one: "I've been a bride boss."

Chapter 9
BE MY GUEST

It doesn't matter who you invite to your wedding. People you don't invite will show up anyway, if they want to be there. A save-the-date postcard, formal invitation, or RSVP card not arriving in their mailbox won't stop that.

Annette warns me that I might have to call security, or at least that's what I think she says. But when I ask her what number I should put in my phone, so when I'm ready for backup I can just press the speed dial button, she corrects me, fast.

"Oh, no, Jen." Her hand grabs my shoulder. "You are security."

Annette slaps a stack of paper and a highlighter into my palms and tells me only the names written down are allowed in. Everyone else has to be shown the exit door.

"But, wait!" I yell after her as she walks back to the bridal suite. "What if they don't listen? What if they came all the way to New Jersey from another country? What if they cry?"

"Only the list, Jen!"

9. BE MY GUEST

The problem with Annette's wedding isn't that she was wishy-washy with who she wanted to invite. It was that other people in her life had a guest list of their own. Annette and her fiancé invited seventy-five people. But her mom went ahead and printed a set of invitations and sent them to an unapproved list of fifty people. Her mother-in-law sent a Paperless Post evite to her own unapproved list of sixty-five people.

By the time Annette found out, the wedding was two weeks away, and screaming fights, long phone calls, and enough tears to almost have irreversible water damage on her iPhone weren't enough to stop all the uninvited guests from booking flights, booking hotel rooms, and passing on the information that they'd like chicken, not fish.

But today is Annette's wedding day, and this isn't her problem anymore. It is mine.

I take my spot at a podium, feet away from the reception hall, with the sacred guest list in hand. I feel like a bouncer from Studio 54, except I am not picking and choosing who is allowed in based on bribes, outfit choices, or the stinging sounds of begs and pleas. I am letting in only the people the bride and groom want there.

"I'm sorry," I say to a group of ten who have arrived together. "None of you are on the guest list. I can't let you into the wedding."

Finally the Bride

"Who do you think you are?" a guy with a skinny bow tie belts out. "I'm the groom's second cousin! My family is inside, and we're going in!"

He signals to the group to follow him and starts to walk around me, straight toward the party doors.

"No! Stop! You can't go in there!"

I have one job right now as the bride's hired bridesmaid, and I can't fail at it. The bride is paying me enough to cover my rent for the month. If her wedding is flooded with the people she told me not to let in, there goes my cash and my reputation as the person who can handle all the dirty work of a wedding.

I run to the door and shield it by making an X shape with my body.

"No. You're not going in here."

The second cousin, who needs to be twice removed from this party, tries to get around me. He tries to push the door open. I won't move.

As soon as the group backs away to call a family member already inside, I go back to my spot at the podium, straighten out my dress, and take a deep breath.

"Next!" I say, as if this is a line at the DMV.

"Sorry, you're not on the list either."

"You were not invited by the bride or the groom."

9. BE MY GUEST

"I understand, but this is a direct order from the couple getting married. You can't go inside."

"The bride can't come to the podium right now. She's getting married!"

"An after-party? I have no idea what the guest list looks like for that."

"No, the open bar is closed to people not on this main guest list."

"Sure, you can call the cops. But I don't think they will care about a person trying to crash a wedding reporting that they aren't allowed in."

"Call security? You're looking at security!"

"Ma'am, please step away from the podium."

I am exhausted by the end of the night.

I have drinks poured on me, a collection of spit sticking to my forehead from people yelling so close to my face, and lots of verbal threats ringing in my ears. But by the time the wedding officially starts, nobody has been let inside that isn't supposed to be there.

As I work more and more weddings as a bridesmaid for hire, I take on many roles just like this one.

I have to take on the role of being a bodyguard at many weddings, scanning the room and making sure uninvited ex-friends, ex-family members, or even ex-lovers are stopped at the front door before they make their grand entrance. At

Finally the Bride

almost every wedding I work, I am handed a file of photos of a person they want me to watch out for because that is the person they have a feeling will show up, even though their name is never on the guest list. About 75% of the time, they are right. That person rolls up, parks their car, and tries to enter the party.

I once saved a wedding by catching a sneaky ex-girlfriend as she pulled up to the valet. I opened her car door and told her it was a better idea for her to drive home than interrupt the wedding. She buckled her seatbelt and turned the car around. What was she here to do? Poison the groom's drink? Interrupt the first dance with a monologue about how awful the groom was to her? Pour red wine on the bride's dress? Luckily, we'll never know.

I thought I had already known the number one lesson of putting together a wedding guest list, but I actually learned, through all of my experiences on the job, the very opposite to be true.

It's not about carefully selecting who you invite; it's about preparing to deal with the wedding crashers from your deep past who pick this day to finally show up and creep back into your life.

You get a glimpse of what that's like the day you get engaged.

9. BE MY GUEST

People crawl out from all different wooded areas of your life, congratulating you and sharing their excitement for the big day.

"I can't wait to celebrate with you and Andrew!"

It's Adam, I want to text back, but instead I mostly send a heart emoji followed by a series of exclamation points. It is my way of delaying the inevitable—figuring out how to make a guest list that doesn't give me anxiety juxtaposed with how to let down all the people who assume they'll be reuniting with me on the dance floor after *so so so* many years.

A lot of these messages come from people I haven't spoken to in a very long time, people I haven't hugged hello in far too long, even though they don't live more than a few blocks away, and people who I wish had picked up the phone and called more, but years have gone by without hearing their voice.

Hearing from them makes me feel this off-balance concoction of elated and deflated.

Why do people wait for big news to say hello? Why do they think of weddings as a time to rekindle relationships? What about all the time in between?

It is in that moment, looking through texts and social media messages, that I realize deciding who will be front row at this wedding and who will watch it from the cheap seats

Finally the Bride

(a.k.a. viewing it from a photo album on Facebook or a wedding montage video cut up for Instagram) will be one of the most grueling decisions I'll have to make.

Which is why I don't make it.

I do try, though.

The first guest list I make only has ten people on it.

My list is mostly empty because I get engaged during a time when there is a lot of friction in my life. I am feeling frustrated by almost everyone. You know the times you go into your closet and feel like you have nothing to wear, but right in front of you are more clothes than the clearance section at Macy's? That's sort of how I feel with the people in my life.

They exist, but they don't fit into my life.

I have family I never speak to and friends who invited me to their weddings years ago but will hardly return my phone calls these days. I don't want to feel like my wedding is packed with people I have to invite because we share a relative or a collection of memories that have expired.

But it doesn't matter how many times you promise you won't invite some of those people, when you finally sit down with a blank sheet of paper and a pen, you write down their names somewhere on the list.

I find myself making three separate lists:

List one: People I want to 100% invite—no questions asked

9. BE MY GUEST

List two: People I think I want to invite, but I'm not sure

List three: I'm leaning toward no, but I can be swayed

Every day, for weeks, I move names around like I am reorganizing furniture, except the feng shui of it all feels so completely off.

Which is why one day all the names and lists are gone, except for ten people.

"You're just inviting ten people to this wedding?" Adam asks, eyeballing the paper I handed him.

"Mhmm, yep," I say casually while washing a pile of dishes longer than the guest list.

Adam's eyebrows stay arched for a while. He is careful not to say anything back. He is either terrified I'll explode or certain that I am doing the right thing. Maybe, after all I've seen at weddings, I am right about not having that 5'7" long guest list that makes weddings feel more squeamish than they have to be.

Careful that I am not making a mistake, I ask the Finally the Bride voters two important questions:

Is there anyone you regret inviting?

Is there anyone you wished you invited that you didn't?

The results: 76% of people say yes, they invited people they wished they didn't, and 91% of people say they regret not inviting someone they wished was there.

Finally the Bride

Which makes me wonder why it's so easy to give an invite to a person you feel like you have to but don't really want there, yet so hard to know who you're leaving out that you will later wish you didn't.

"Invite them all," a friend of mine says over cappuccinos one August afternoon. "It will be less regretful if you just hand out invites like Oprah gave out cars."

What would that even look like? If I invite everyone on all three of my lists, my guest count will be 200 (not including Adam's list). It will feel like a jumbled personal reunion.

"But that's what weddings are for," my mom reminds me, her wisdom entering my guest list decision-making process. "These parties are excuses for family to see each other again."

She is right. We do have the kind of family that only sees each other when someone gets married or someone dies. We are all either hugging and laughing or hugging and crying. The years between big life events are spent apart, often in silence.

I know I'd regret not inviting family over friends. I ask my mom to write a list of the family members who should be there. I decide to trust her decision on every name she puts down.

But when it comes to friends, I make the instant decision that the names not on my 100% list are not getting an invitation.

9. BE MY GUEST

I hand over my final list to Adam, including my original ten names of friends and my mom's list of our family members. We send out save the dates and close out the guest list decision.

I can't help but think about that guy who almost charged the door and took me down with it at Annette's wedding.

Why did he want to get in so badly?

Was it that he wanted his share of free food and drink? Was it that he felt he belonged? Was it that he took weddings to be family reunions?

There are plenty of moments to catch up, get coffee, go for a walk, or have a phone call. But that shouldn't just be what a wedding is for, though oftentimes it is, and your guest list looks like a phonebook of people's numbers you hardly ever think to call.

Even as I write that, I still feel bubbles popping in my stomach.

"Do you feel like you should have invited anyone else?" Adam asks, months after sending out the save the dates.

At first, I wonder if I made a mistake. But as the days go on, it feels like I did the right thing.

Have you ever found yourself roaming a shoe store with a pair in your hand unsure if it's worth swiping your credit card for them? So you leave them, walk out, and promise to go back days later if your gut tells you that you made the wrong decision, but you never do. You just never do.

It is all, sort of, just like that.

Chapter 10
MY BIG FAT DIVORCE

"Do you actually want to get married?" my therapist asks me as I sit back on her flower-patterned fabric couch, the stress sweat now seeping out of my shirt and onto her furniture.

The thing I love the most about my therapist is when she interrupts me mid-sentence and asks the very question I'm working so hard to avoid answering.

"I don't want to get divorced," I reply, hoping that is the golden ticket that will get me out of this conversation.

We had been talking about my worries about marriage years before I was engaged. But now that I have a ring on my finger and save the dates postmarked, the conversations feel more unfiltered.

My therapist doesn't say anything back. So we both listen to the buzz of a mosquito circling the office until she swats it with her hand and the mosquito flies underneath the couch. I look down at the bug, wishing we could trade places.

Finally the Bride

"It's just, I've seen a lot, and I'm scared of getting married because what if one day it falls apart and I lose everything."

"Everything?"

"Everything, like my independence, my money, my life goals!"

"But what if you don't get divorced? What if you don't lose everything?"

"But what if I do?"

Our session ends, and as she guides me out the front door of her office, she asks that I think through the logic behind this fear.

"Ask yourself if you're more excited about getting married or more scared about the possibility of getting divorced."

The next day, I meet a divorce lawyer by accident.

"Do you have a backup plan?" she asks me after noticing my sparkling engagement ring after a workout class.

"A backup plan? Like, for the wedding?"

"No, for your life if you get divorced."

She lifts my hand, twirls my ring, and says she's seen people just like me before.

"Woman about to get married with no idea what marriage actually means."

"To have and to hold? For richer or poorer?" I ask.

"Yeah, the rich and poor part is mostly when it all falls apart."

10. MY BIG FAT DIVORCE

The woman digs into her purse, pulls out a card, leaves it in my palm.

"Call me when you want to talk about the P-word."

The truth is, I've never heard anyone talk about prenups before.

My parents never mentioned the word, and the countless friends that have gotten married before me never brought it up.

It is a taboo word that doesn't enter the conversations I find myself in. It isn't something I ask people about either. How would that conversation go? Over brunch, in between mimosa refills, the casual ask for everyone at the table to raise their hand if they got a prenup? It seems personal, private, and pretentious to bring up. Plus, I assume none of my friends have one, until finally, I ask them.

Most say no. One says yes.

"I was getting ready for the ceremony, and my husband walked in the room and handed me a pile of papers," she admits. "He asked me to sign them on the spot. The ceremony was about to start. I was in utter shock."

"Tell me you didn't sign it."

"I signed without looking."

"But were you scared you signed your life away? Were you mad?"

Finally the Bride

"Mad yes, scared no. I realized love is sticky until it isn't anymore and slides away. If that day comes, I know now what the end of our marriage will look like. There's a weird calmness in knowing that."

I know that divorce and prenups are something I need to talk to Adam about. But how do you bring those topics up to a person who just got on a knee and asked to spend the rest of their life with you? How do you casually say, "Hey! Let's meet with a divorce lawyer and plan the way this all ends, if it does ever end, so your wife-to-be can sleep at night"?

I decide to ask Livia DeFilippis Barndollar, who has more than thirty-five years of experience ably representing parties in dissolution of marriage cases and shares that talking about money is a must before getting married, though it's not easy.

"Talking about money can be hard because certain families and cultures often consider discussions about money to be invasive," says Barndollar.

"Determining how to handle money and how to make money decisions is, however, integral to your lives together as a married couple and should be had, whether it has to do with prenups or not."

When I finally bring up the topic of a prenup and a meeting with a divorce lawyer to Adam, six months after he pops the marriage question, he nearly spits tomato soup all over the table.

10. MY BIG FAT DIVORCE

"Marriage makes me scared," I say as he looks at me with eager eyes.

"What's going on?" he asks, unsure how I had gone from talking about catering pizza at our wedding to seeming like I am questioning our future together.

"We should talk about protecting our money," I say. "We should talk about how to walk away without a giant mess, if it comes to that."

"I don't understand," he finally responds. "Why are we planning for the worst when we haven't even lived the best yet?"

Adam has known me for five years, and one of the things I adore the most about him is how he often forgets about the pessimistic and worrisome characteristics that he has none of and I have too much of sometimes.

"It's just that I need to know if we fall out of love . . ."

"We're not going to fall out of love."

"But the divorce lawyer said people do all the time!"

After explaining to Adam that I didn't secretly meet with a divorce lawyer and just had a brief interaction with one in a workout class, I tell him that I would, indeed, like to meet with a divorce lawyer.

"Go if you want," he says. "I just don't want to be part of this."

Finally the Bride

A couple of weeks later, I enter a fancy office building on Fifth Avenue for my appointment with the divorce lawyer who had handed me her card, and I confess I have no idea why I'm there.

"I'm just scared of this marriage thing and want to know what changes and what's different when I sign on the dotted line of my marriage license and lock lives with my partner."

"You're smart for being here," she says, telling me about how most people don't think that way before they tie the knot. Even though she's a strong believer in marriage and love, the facts are facts, and the fact is, not every couple will spend their life together forever.

She spends an hour with me breaking down four main things to think about, chat about, and decide on before walking down the aisle.

I'm going to share them with you now.

- **Health Rights**

Before we talk about money, I first ask what else changes when people get married legally? She mentions health-care rights. For example, when you are legally married, you can join your spouse's health insurance plan. But also, when an emergency happens, health-care professionals can turn to your spouse for decisions when you can't make them yourself.

10. MY BIG FAT DIVORCE

This is a conversation you should have with your partner before getting married so that you can get on the same page about medical procedures in case of an emergency. You can protect yourself legally by either making this person your health-care agent (also known as your proxy) or create a living will to protect yourself and clearly define your treatment preferences in case of an emergency.

- **Taxes**

The next topic that comes to the table fits perfectly with a topic I often roll my eyes at solo—taxes. Once married, she reminds me, you have the option of filing your taxes jointly.

But you don't have to. While filing joint returns has benefits, like deductions and tax credits that could lower your tax bracket, sometimes filing individually can be a better option to lower your tax bill.

What's also important to know, as a potential protection, if you're married and file separately, you only claim responsibility for your own return and may not be liable for your spouse's taxes and penalties, even if you later divorce.

- **Money**

When it comes time to talk about money, I tell her that we have already taken steps to protect our money by deciding to keep a few personal bank accounts separate once we get married to use for our own purchases and decisions.

She instantly presses the pause button and explains a big misconception that a lot of couples have before getting married.

"There are legal rights that are acquired in the financial state," she says. "The day before you're married, if your soon-to-be spouse earns income, that is their money. The day after you're married, any income they earn becomes marital money."

My mouth opens. I had assumed that the money I earned was money in my name only. I was wrong.

"People think they can get married and keep separate bank accounts, but that's not true," she says, explaining that every dollar you now make becomes marital, and when you comingle accounts or assets you had premarriage, they now become marital.

So how to protect your assets before marriage? That's when she recommends a prenup or establishing bank accounts, before you get married, which you can withdraw money from but can't add any new money to. That way it doesn't become marital.

10. MY BIG FAT DIVORCE

- **Prenup**

Finally, the hot topic surfaces about getting a prenup. I tell her that this isn't something my partner and I need to get because we don't have a lot of money or assets.

She's heard that before. "Some people will say, 'I don't need a prenup. I have "nothing,"' meanwhile they have bank accounts and retirement accounts," she says. "When the divorce rate is around 50%, divorce and prenups should be normalized. At the end of the day, marriage is a legal business relationship, so we need to be practical, and getting a prenup can strengthen a marriage."

The thought of doing a prenup with my partner feels like something that could shake up our relationship and not strengthen it, so I ask the divorce lawyer why.

"Getting a prenup allows a couple to talk about things more than money, often where people stand with money and even things about their past," she says. "Plus, you strengthen how you speak to each other and maybe even have a breakthrough moment."

I wonder what the conversation with a lawyer would look like. Does the couple sit down and pour out how much they love each other and then start negotiating who gets what if the marriage ends? *What an oxymoron of a situation*, I think.

Finally the Bride

She explains that when she sits down with a couple, she can handle the prenup however they'd like and then walk them through what the worst-case scenario would look like regarding their money and assets in case of a divorce.

After my talk with the divorce lawyer, I walk fifty blocks home, think about everything she said, and hug Adam real tightly when I open the door.

"I'm more excited about the idea of marriage than I am the fear of divorce."

He hugs me back, sighs like he's done a million times before, and finally says he is excited too, though worried I am having second thoughts.

"No, my thoughts aren't the issue. But having these conversations that no one tells you to talk about is the issue."

People will call all of this unromantic. People will think meeting a divorce lawyer before marriage is bad luck. But what if it was more normal? What if it was a requirement? What if we stopped viewing our relationships like rom-coms where there is always a happy ending? What if we viewed it as what it is—*a legally binding decision that impacts your life*?

Speaking with a divorce lawyer before getting married educates us about what actually changes after the giant party ends and we go off on our honeymoon as officially wed. Does

10. MY BIG FAT DIVORCE

having these conversations make our relationship awkward? Yes, but for only a few minutes. We're still deciding if we should get a prenup or even just jot down how we want to handle our finances to protect us both in case something happens.

After we finish having deep conversations about these topics and still continue to talk about getting a prenup, our relationship does feel stronger, and we feel like we have a realistic game plan, for sickness and health, and truly for better or for worse.

"But mostly for the better," Adam adds.

"Of course! *But also for the worse*," I chime in.

Adam rolls his eyes and I roll mine, our negotiated way of agreeing without officially agreeing, *yet*.

Chapter 11

I DON'T WANT TO BE YOUR FRIEND ANYMORE

Days after I told Whitney I'd want her to be my bridesmaid, she told me she never wanted to speak to me again.

I wasn't engaged yet, not even close. Adam and I had only been dating for two years. We had loosely talked about getting married and having a wedding, but it wasn't on our immediate to-do list.

But what triggered me to prematurely ask a friend to get comfy with the idea of being my bridesmaid was that I feared I wouldn't have any by the time I did get married.

I had just worked a 550-person wedding in New Jersey where the bride had fifteen bridesmaids. I grew obsessed with wondering how a person could know so many people. Did they invite all their Facebook acquaintances? Did the local news report the details of their wedding and confirm it was open to the public? Did they give every single person not just a plus one but a plus five?

11. I DON'T WANT TO BE YOUR FRIEND ANYMORE

The wedding was so big that they had multiple dance floors, open bars, and buffet stations. It felt more like a party for an entire small city than any kind of intimate wedding.

Before the wedding started, I asked the bride every question I could think of.

How do you both know that many people?

Isn't it going to cost a fortune?

Are all these people on your guest list people you want to invite or have to invite?

Seriously though, how do you have all of these best friends? I hardly have two!

The bride looked at me like I was the crazy one.

"Jen, our original guest list was 850. We cut it down quite a bit. I asked twenty-five people to be my bridesmaid, and these are just the ones who said yes. Trust me, whenever you finally get engaged, you'll see how hard it is not to have a massive guest list and bridal party."

I knew deep down that wasn't true. I was never the kind of person who surrounded myself with crowds of people. I was painfully shy growing up. I skipped the playground for solo reading sessions in the library. I cried so much at sleepovers that my dad always had to come pick me up (this usually meant that the new friend who had invited me over never wanted to invite me again). I was bullied in middle school for looking, sounding, and acting differently than the other

Finally the Bride

girls at my small private school, and bullied even more for caring about things they didn't (like the Rolling Stones instead of S Club 7). I had friends in my young years, but never best friends.

The same was true now. I had graduated from my early twenties, a time in life when you're still holding on to the friends from your college days, and I noticed that the group I had forced myself to fit in with for so many of my adult years was scattering without me. Many of the people who had me stand up straight with a bouquet of flowers in my hands for their wedding would now laugh at me if I asked them to be a bridesmaid in mine. We were growing apart. Time had passed, and it would keep passing before I'd get engaged. I feared I'd have no one left to ask to be a bridesmaid.

But I felt an urge to both prove that bride wrong and prove myself right—that even if my bridesmaid list was small, it was because those on it were people I truly adored.

Which is why I decided to sit down and make a list.

I'm going to show this bride that not every single person has a ton of friends that can just magically morph into bridesmaids.

I emailed the bride my list of three names and said, "See, look! Not everyone has a ton of friends! Not everyone is so popular like you."

She never replied back, and I started to feel self-conscious. I started to judge myself. Was my tiny, yet mighty, list of

11. I DON'T WANT TO BE YOUR FRIEND ANYMORE

three names an indication that I had failed in life? By now, should I have a cluster of friends to parade around with from all areas of my life to show people that I had succeeded in a human skill people assume is easy—making friends? Would guests at my wedding raise their brows when three people walked down the aisle as my bridesmaids and keep looking back at the door wondering where everyone else was?

All of this made me nervous enough to want to start confirming with my friends, now, that they'd be available to be my bridesmaid later, *whenever that would be.*

That's how I found myself, on a drizzly Friday night, sitting outside a pizza restaurant deep inside an up-and-coming neighborhood of Brooklyn, facing Whitney, desperate to get all of this off my chest.

"I did something today I probably shouldn't have."

"What did you do now, Jen?" Whitney replied, as if my uncanny antics were starting to make her skin crawl.

Whitney and I had been friends for close to ten years, enough time to know the inside out intricacies of a person, like how they sound when they sneeze or how many bites of pizza it takes to finish a single slice (spoiler alert: no more than five for me). She knew most of my secrets, mistakes, and embarrassing mishaps that took three shots of tequila to admit to anyone else.

Finally the Bride

So when I told her I had done something odd, she probably assumed I had texted an ex-boyfriend, *again,* snooped through Adam's phone, or submitted paperwork to adopt a dog, even though my landlord made it clear the building didn't allow pets. But it wasn't any of those things, and Whitney began to twist her body in a way that signaled she wanted me to get to the point.

"I made a list of who I'd want as my bridesmaids."

"But you're not . . ."

"Yeah, I know. But at this wedding I worked, the bride had a bridal party bigger than a sorority! I just wanted to think through who I'd even ask, and it's not enough people to even play a game of poker!"

I shoved my phone in front of her face so she could see for herself.

She instantly handed it back. I didn't know it then, but I know it now—Whitney was looking for any excuse to exhale closer and closer toward the finish line of our friendship. People always ask when you break up with a significant other if you saw it coming; the answer is usually yes. But nobody ever asks about a friendship breakup, and the truth is, you hardly see it coming because you take all the red flags, the smoke signals, as the person just having a bad day, not having bad feelings toward you.

11. I DON'T WANT TO BE YOUR FRIEND ANYMORE

I wish I saw what Whitney was wanting me to see—her discomfort, her angst, her "I'm so over this, Jen"—and she was making it clear. Her elbow was on the table, and her chin was in her hands. She was clearly scrolling through text messages with other people. Her eyes were anywhere but near mine.

I wish I saw all of that because what I did next just made me feel extremely foolish days later.

"And just so you know, you're going to be my bridesmaid. That's a no-brainer!"

Whitney's eyebrows morphed into sideways question marks, and before she could answer, the rain started up again, making our pizza soggy. Whitney jumped up, grabbed to-go boxes, and said we should call it a night.

"Okay, talk later, bye," she said, zooming off to her nearby apartment, not inviting me over, not willing to spend the rest of the night hearing about my bridesmaid dilemma for a wedding that didn't exist.

I didn't think much of it. It was already 8 pm, and I didn't mind making my way home and putting an end to this nonsense of a problem I was hooked on solving. Figuring out who my bridesmaids would be wasn't something I needed to do until I needed to do it. I was over it, for now. I grabbed my things and my soggy slice of pizza and hailed a cab home.

Days later, Whitney started to casually ignore my texts. Monday would turn into Friday, and I wouldn't hear a thing from her. Soon after, I begged her to meet me in person. I wanted to hash this out and find out what was going on. She finally agreed, and on a Tuesday afternoon, we met on the corner of Twenty-First and Broadway, just so she could stare at the gum-stained sidewalk and utter a sentence I'll never be able to forget.

"Jen, I don't want to be your friend anymore."

"Is this about being my bridesmaid? Because you don't have to! You don't have to say yes! Heck, I'm not engaged or anything. It's just that I wanted you to know that you're one of my best friends, and I'd want you to be my future . . ."

"Jen," she cut me off, eager to make sure I was hearing what she was saying one final time. "I just don't want to be your friend anymore."

Her statement didn't come with a thesis. She didn't shower me with explanations or evidence of why she thought I was a horrible friend and wanted to end our ten-year streak of being buddy-buddy. She just said that, turned left, and disappeared into a crowd of lunchtime passersby. I never saw her again.

I've been broken up with by boyfriends more times than I can count on one hand but never by a good friend, and it hurt more than all of those exes combined.

It takes my years to stop thinking about Whitney at least once a day, and finally, I do. But when I get engaged and

11. I DON'T WANT TO BE YOUR FRIEND ANYMORE

people get noisy about who my bridesmaids will be and what kind of dresses they'll wear, the feelings from that Friday night with Whitney begin to pound loudly on my chest.

"So who do you want to be your bridesmaids?" my mom asks, days after getting engaged. We are riding in the car, and I lower the window. The fresh air hits my skin like a blow-dryer, there to force back the onset of tears.

I am embarrassed to answer because I wonder if my mom, like the rest of the world, expects me to rattle off a longer list of people than I have in mind. I have only two names to share, and I question even asking them. What if the question makes them run away? What if they pull a Whitney?

"I don't want bridesmaids," I say, staring up at the puffy clouds.

"What! How can the bridesmaid for hire not have bridesmaids?"

"The bridesmaid for hire, Mom, feels like she doesn't have enough friends."

That's the thing about wedding planning, it makes you feel like you're constantly not enough. Like you don't have enough money to afford your wish list of things you pinned on Pinterest, not enough friends to fill a bridal entourage, not enough days to get in picture-perfect shape even though you thought you were happy with your body, and not enough

Finally the Bride

time to do all the things listed on every suggested bridal to-do list.

As the pressure sinks in, the person getting married does whatever they can to feel enough. They take out loans, max out credit cards, find personal trainers, and commit to unhealthy diet plans. That's one reason people come to me and hire their bridesmaids.

Early on, I had a bride phone me from Detroit in need of having me at her wedding because she didn't have any friends to ask to be her bridesmaid.

"Not one?" I asked.

"Not one."

When I told people about that, they laughed! They called her names!

What a loser. Who doesn't have a friend? I don't believe that. Can't she ask a cousin?

But what people don't understand is that not everybody has a girl squad, a friend group, a Rolodex of people to call up from all different parts of their lives. If you do have that, consider it rare. Most people have friends to go to happy hour with, grab Sunday brunch with, or text back and forth with a few times a month, but not everyone has best friends.

The truth is, one in four people do not have any close friends.

Perhaps there's nothing odd, weird, or strange about that. Perhaps those people grew apart from friends over the years

11. I DON'T WANT TO BE YOUR FRIEND ANYMORE

and have been swarmed with other pressing things in life than finding new friends. Or maybe they are just picky. Maybe they only want friends who are loyal and understanding. The older I get, the faster I learn how hard it is to meet people like that.

Just because our social media feeds are Slip 'N Slides of pictures of people having these gigantic bachelorette parties, where everyone is wearing a matching one-piece swimsuit and cheersing with mini bottles of champagne, doesn't mean we need to have a copy and paste of that in our own lives to feel validated, to fit in, to feel enough.

I remember being back in high school where people showed off their popularity on their birthdays: as friends would arrive in the morning, each would hand them a birthday balloon. You'd lug these balloons around all day, and people would stare in awe. The more balloons you had, the more you were crowned popular. One girl, Brittany, had a record of 100 balloons for her birthday. She needed five other people to stand behind her all day and carry the balloons around. The most I ever got was eighteen, but it was one of the best days of my life because I felt loved and cared about—*finally.*

Birthday balloons back then felt a whole lot like how having a big bridal party feels now. Yet, I can see it all for what it really is—a deflated way of proving a perception of yourself that's not wholeheartedly true. It's just what everyone else expects to see because they've grown used to seeing it.

Let me tell you a secret about those balloons. One year, I bought all of my own. I was worried people would forget or that I didn't have as many friends as I thought. So I woke up early on my birthday, begged my mom to take me to CVS, and walked to school with as many balloons as I could carry. I went from feeling invisible to feeling extraordinary, just for the day.

I always ask people who hire me, the ones who will also have real friends in the bridal party, how they decide who to ask. These are the most common reasons I hear:

I'm asking this person because I don't have a choice. I have to.

I'm asking this person because if I don't, there will be too much drama.

I'm asking this person because I want more than five bridesmaids.

I'm asking this person because she asked me a few years ago and I have to return the favor.

I'm asking this person because I want it to repair our friendship. Spoiler alert: it never really does.

I'm asking this person because we're lifelong friends. This one is rare but beautiful.

I'm asking this person because I hope she'll say yes.

11. I DON'T WANT TO BE YOUR FRIEND ANYMORE

It's like the only role of a bridesmaid is to show you proof you have friends. Dress them up in polyester, get their hair curled, and hand them a stack of flowers. Let them walk down the aisle so your guests can nod their heads and check off the box that says, Wow, Jen has friends!

It starts to feel so jumbled and unimportant. I am lucky to have two incredible friends. I don't need to prove something to anyone, or myself.

The same day I'm alone in the car with my mom and she's asking me who my bridesmaids will be, a text message pops up on my phone from a person I never thought I'd hear from again.

It's Whitney.

"Hey, Jen. Saw you got engaged! Congrats to you and Adam. Wishing you the best!"

I instantly start writing back. It has been years, but I have so much to say:

You were supposed to be my bridesmaid, ya know? It sucks. I wish you cared. I'm sorry if I hurt you, but look, I still miss you, and I want you to be my bridesmaid . . .

I roll the window down even lower. I open my mouth to suck down some fresh oxygen that I hope will travel to my brain and shake me out of making a mistake I don't want to make.

Finally the Bride

I erase everything I had typed.

Why was I going to beg someone to come back into my life? Friendships are not meant to last forever. Nothing in life is forever. People come together and break apart for so many reasons. Weddings are one of the only times in a person's life where they feel like they have to take inventory of their friend situation, brush the dust off of old relationships, and parade around with a crew of people.

I write Whitney back only two words. The only words I truly mean.

Thank you.

And I mean them because when someone exits your life, you have to let them go. Just like the balloons that once brought me so much joy, they too whittle down to nothingness. Friendships are good when they are good, but when they're over, I've learned, let them be over.

What matters, at any time of your life, isn't who is available to show up for one moment, one day, one celebration, but who will be there even after the open bar closes, the dance floor is swept clean, and the dirty bridesmaid dress is tossed to the back of a closet. What matters the most is who is left standing when it's all over.

Not how many people.

Chapter 12

MONEY TALKS BUT I TALK BACK

Very few things are more awkward for me to talk about than the topic of money.

I can talk about pooping and the intricate details of getting my period without my cheeks turning red. But ask me how we should fairly split the bill at brunch or the best way to combine our life's savings when we one day get married, and I will pretend I forgot how to speak.

I blame all of this on you, Steve Kantor.

If you're reading this, I want to settle something once and for all: I don't owe you a penny. I never did in the first place.

Steve Kantor was my best friend in high school. He lived down the street, and we spent a lot of time watching teen drama movies and trying to write jokes. He used to call me "Punchline" because when his jokes would fall flat, I'd step in and rewrite the ending. I used to call him "Yawn" because I never thought any of his jokes were that funny. But Steve was one of the only friends I had where I didn't feel the pressure to be anybody but myself. His friendship meant the world to me.

One lazy after-school-noon, I told Steve that there was no expiration date on our friendship. I hoped it'd last forever. Steve looked at me, smiled, and said, "We're Gouda friends. Gotta keep it cheesy!" and we laughed until our faces ached.

Steve was on the student council and the only junior invited to senior prom that year. When he asked me to go with him, it felt like getting backstage access to our entire high school hierarchy of popularity. Being one of two juniors at the prom felt like the best way to bump me up toward semi-cool. At the time, I was holding on to being known as the nice but weird Jen. I wanted to be the nice and cool Jen. I couldn't say no.

I dug through my wallet and scraped together enough of my babysitting cash to cover the cost of my ticket and forked it over to Steve.

"I got this, Jen," he said. "It's my treat."

"No way! I worked hard for this $97, and I want it to go toward my share of our adventure crashing the senior prom."

Steve folded up my clump of cash and stuck it back in my hand.

"We're good," he said. "Just bring $97 worth of dance moves, and we're even."

12. MONEY TALKS BUT I TALK BACK

I didn't know it then, but Steve, for the first time in our friendship, was serious.

I figured this out the morning after prom when I looked at my phone only to see a text from Steve:

"You owe me $97. Leave it in my mailbox. Thanks."

I took a few seconds to rub my eyes and read it again before responding:

"Once again, your punchline is crappy. Try again with this joke!"

"Not a joke. Give me my money."

"Huh?"

"I took you to prom, and you spent the whole night hanging out with everyone but me. I thought we'd at least kiss."

"WHAT IS GOING ON, STEVE? A kiss? We're friends, ew. Also, since when do you care about any of this stuff?"

"Jen, give me the $97 back. You owe it to me."

Turns out Steve had expectations for that night, and one of those expectations was that I was supposed to read his mind. He had never told me he liked me like that, and even so, I didn't owe him anything that night, not even a refund because I wasn't the date of his miscommunicated dreams.

I didn't give him the cash back, and Steve never spoke to me again.

Finally the Bride

The end of our friendship, over not returning money I didn't feel I owed, haunted me more than I ever imagined it would.

Not just because Steve wouldn't let it go. He never spoke directly to me again, but our senior year, someone taped up a poster that said "Nobody ask Jen Glantz to prom." I knew it was Steve. For years, I'd get emails from a random person with no subject line and nothing inside except for the number 97. One time, I saw someone had written a review of my book and had only written, "Not worth reading. Save your $97 and spend it on someone else."

But ever since then, when the topic of money came up on a first date, I became skeevish.

A lot of people will tell you a lot of things about how to approach handling the bill on a first date. Some will say the person who set up the date should pay for it.

Others will say it's best to avoid offering at all costs, even if the bill sits on the table and hours go by without anyone paying it.

But perhaps the best advice I could never follow came from a friend who said that when she senses the bill is about to come, she gets up and heads to the bathroom. Once she's back, if it's not taken care of, she'll dig for her wallet and offer.

I ignored all of this, always.

12. MONEY TALKS BUT I TALK BACK

I usually opened up my entire wallet and put down my debit card and a stuck-to-it coupon to Bed Bath & Beyond. If they slid my card back to me, I always insisted that they at least keep the coupon.

"These things don't expire," I'd say with the utmost amount of pride.

I felt better about the situation as a bill grabber because, most of the time, I meant it, especially if it was equal. But on some dates, I found myself trying to heal old wounds of not wanting to owe anyone anything by paying for bills that were extraordinarily unfair.

Once, I ordered a glass of ginger ale, and the person I was on a first date with ordered a steak and a bottle of wine. The little cartoon image of Steve danced in my head, saying, *Jen, you better offer to pay for this, all of this, or else!* So when the bill came, I frisbee-tossed my card on the table, and the guy said, "Great, thanks, Jen," leaving me to take care of the $120 tab, making that the most expensive glass of ginger ale in the entire world.

Adam and I talk about everything, but when we talk about money, I get weird.

Even after dating for five years, whenever he pays for something that's expensive, I find an urge to sneak him back the money. As if I fear one day, he too will wake up and demand I owe some sort of refund on our relationship.

Finally the Bride

I know that's not true because Adam isn't like that; he's never been like that. Even when we started dating, he never asked me to pay him back for anything, and as we spent more time together, things just became natural in the money department. We took turns paying for dinner, went 50/50 on adventures, and never kept track of who bought what. We didn't have much of a game plan for keeping tabs on who bought what, but when you're with someone for a while, things just even out. The only things we religiously split were our rent and utilities. But with everything else, the line of who paid for what blurred into the background of our lives together.

Money wasn't an awkward thing to talk about, until we got engaged.

"We, umm, have to talk about money," I shared, weeks after he popped the question and our brains were melting inside the intricacies of wedding-planning spreadsheets.

"What about money?"

"Well, don't we have to talk about merging all of our dollars together in some great big pot that we share and take from?"

I only said that because I had read a checklist on the internet about things people should do when they get engaged, and it said, "Merge finances with your fiancé." I figured the faster we talked about this, the less awkward it would be.

12. MONEY TALKS BUT I TALK BACK

I also did that because years ago, my co-worker Samantha had come walking into the office crying one day because she and her husband had combined their finances, and he had stolen all of their money and had run off with someone he matched with on Plenty of Fish.

"I want to talk about this because we have to decide what we're going to do about merging our money," I explained to Adam. "But also because I want to make sure I have my own cash available in case one day our relationship tragically ends."

"Okay, well, I don't see it ever ending," Adam said. "But in any case, what should we do? Should we combine everything?"

"I don't know!" I lashed out, letting my personal fears and trepidations corrupt the conversation. "You tell me!"

We decided that before we made any decisions, we'd sit down together and talk about how much money we each spend every month and then try to settle on a joint budget.

But that idea failed fast.

Minutes into us taking inventory of our past bank statements and agreeing on some sort of budget, we got into the kind of heated argument that just doesn't have any kind of cool solution.

"Let's keep everything separate and never talk about this again!"

"Jen, let's get some help."

Finally the Bride

I thought Adam meant, Let's go see a couple's therapist, so I was shocked when, a few days later, I met him in Midtown Manhattan to sit down with a financial advisor instead.

"So what's it going to be, Jonathan?" I said to the finance guy, pacing nervously around his office like I'd just downed six shots of espresso.

Jonathan had spent a while analyzing our finances, separately, and looking over our polar opposite ideas for joint budgets.

"Well, here's what I think . . ."

But before Jonathan could lend his professional advice, I burst into a minute-long monologue over how I just didn't want to combine all of my money with all of Adam's money.

"I don't want to fight about money. I don't want to argue over the fact that Adam spends $25 more a day on food than I do. I don't want to not have bank accounts of my own that I can use how I'd like or save in case of an emergency. I don't want to ever feel like I owe anyone a penny. I owe that to myself! I don't want any of this."

"Jen, why do you think you need to do anything differently than you're already doing with Adam?" Jonathan asked in the kindest of ways, which made me wonder if he was secretly also a marriage therapist.

"Because isn't that what couples do when they get married? Isn't that what everyone does?"

12. MONEY TALKS BUT I TALK BACK

"Says who?"

"My pre-marriage to-do list that I downloaded from online!"

Jonathan's eyebrows curved upward. He hit the table with our piles of financial papers and set us straight.

"Stop listening to outdated advice, Jen," Jonathan said. "It's 2020. When it comes to money, do what works for the two of you. Not what anyone else does or has done in the past."

Jonathan spent the rest of the hour with us talking about how we could set up a joint account for split purchases (like rent and shared bills) and how we could also maintain our own accounts to pay for what we'd like.

Dealing with finances isn't a one-size-fits-all approach. Neither is any issue in a relationship. But sometimes the internet roundups or the couples you ask for advice will tell you differently. Just because everyone you know combined their finances before they tied the knot doesn't mean you have to follow their lead. Big decisions in relationships are personal and tense but only solvable if both people are open to devising a plan that fits them.

"Keep things how they are, for now, since it's been working out great for the two of you these past five years," he said. "But nothing is permanent, and you can always change how you split up your money and what you merge together."

Finally the Bride

Leaving there, Adam had a big smile on his face, but I'm willing to bet my smile was a whole lot bigger.

I feel safe knowing that we can keep our finances as is, for now, and that getting married won't mess that up. Adam and I talk about money, a lot, and it's comforting to know we can have transparent and honest conversations about a topic that once made my skin crawl. It's not the topic, I've learned, it's the baggage you bring from the past that just makes the topic feel widely more intense than it truly needs to be.

But, there is one more thing I want to admit.

A few years after moving to New York City, I was leaving a workout class in the middle of summer, with the sweat from my messy bun dripping onto my forehead, when I looked up from my phone, and there he was, Steve, after so many years of not seeing him or speaking to him.

I stood still on the sidewalk, searching for a bush or building to hide in while he walked by, but I didn't have time. Steve saw me, his eyes drawn toward mine like magnets that haven't lost their charge. He went pale, like he'd just seen a ghost, except the ghost was his ex-best friend that he owed at least 97 apologies to. But in true Steve fashion, he didn't say a word. He walked right by me as if pretending that he didn't know me would erase the fact that he did.

I turned back to see him still staring, and in an effort to give what I truly think I owed, I danced as wacky and as

12. MONEY TALKS BUT I TALK BACK

wildly as I could until he crossed the street and faded into the Manhattan skyline.

Let me tell you, that performance was worth way more than $97, but at this point, let's just call it even.

Chapter 13

HOW TO CANCEL YOUR WEDDING

STEP ONE: FALL IN LOVE
Fall so madly in love with a person that you're willing to part ways with your independence. Fall so awkwardly and uncannily in love with a person that you're okay with never sleeping alone in your own bed ever again, okay with having another point of view in the mix when you're trying to make dinner decisions, okay with filing your taxes jointly.

You realize, one night while splitting a plate of lasagna, that if you keep falling so madly in love with this person, one day you will be responsible for another person's taxes. Lick a sudden bad taste in your mouth. Ask if the lasagna is burnt. Realize these thoughts just keep burning you.

Fall so in love with a person that you have to tell them to leave. That you show them the door and say, "I love you so much, but I'm scared, just go." Watch as they don't move. Watch as the dirt from your doormat catches on the hallway wind and blows itself out. *Finally, something goes.* Stand still as your left foot tingles. Listen as the door creaks louder than

13. HOW TO CANCEL YOUR WEDDING

the shrieking, manipulative sound in your gut that screams, "Looks like they passed the test!"

Fall so in love with a person that you tell them you never want to get married, that you're the kind of woman who wasn't meant to settle down. Tell them your dreams of growing old in a studio apartment overlooking Central Park. Make mention of a pact you have with your roommate to live together forever, no matter what.

Spend years begging that person to forget you ever said that. Get hysterical when you ask why they haven't proposed yet, and roll your eyes when they say, with the professionalism of a person who is committed to studying you like a textbook, that they were certain you didn't want that because you said, well, you said you didn't.

Talk about marriage as often as you talk about pizza. Bring it up whenever you can. Open to page 57 of a book you rented from the library that shares how some people are nervous about the idea of marriage but they can grow into it. Mention how much you've grown up lately. Hint about a wedding dress you saw inside a shop window. Clap loudly at the end of rom-coms, just like you've seen people do when airplanes land, to reinforce how much you love the idea of love.

Storm out of a coffee shop when he tells you that his best friend got engaged to someone he's known for a year. Throw

Finally the Bride

your hot coffee in the trash and slam the front door three times. That's how many years you've been together. That's how hard you've fallen in love. Confess later how you're jealous. Confess later that you fear you two have switched places. Confess you've found the answers to the questions he's just now asking himself.

Lock yourself in a bathroom when his other friend gets engaged. "It's all happening to everyone else; what about me?" you whisper into the wooden door. "What about us?" Wonder if you put too much pressure on this. Know you put too much pressure on yourself. Accept you've put too much pressure on him too.

Let time pass. Fix the parts of your relationship that have been scattered around like billiard balls on a pool table. Think deeply about the question your therapist asks you: "Do you want to get married, or do you think the world wants you to get married?"

Respond with one word: "Both."

Go to his friends' weddings. Laugh into a glass of champagne about how we have to be happy for other people who have exactly what we want. Talk out loud to yourself one night on a walk around the block about how stubborn you can be, how it's hard for you to admit what you truly want, and how you don't even know what you want, but you do know how in love you are with perhaps the only person in

13. HOW TO CANCEL YOUR WEDDING

this world you'd want to spend your life with in a studio apartment overlooking Central Park.

STEP TWO: SAY THE WORD *YES*

When you find yourself digging your knuckles into your eyelids to make sure you're seeing this correctly, remember to say yes. He's down on a knee, asking you to be his partner on this adventure called life, asking you to marry him. You say yes as many times as you can before your throat gets sore. You spend the rest of the day with a smile that looks like it's tattooed on your face. You spend the rest of the day ignoring what you know is about to come next—a polar vortex of wedding hysteria that you're not nearly as prepared for as you should be.

You make a pact with yourself. For the next week, ignore the calls, hide the texts, turn a shoulder to all questions about what you want to do for your dream wedding. Everyone in your life is tapping their toes, expecting answers, but you just want to celebrate the fact that you fell in love, talked yourself out of falling in love, refused to mess up that love, and now you're here, engaged to this person.

"The rest is just details," you say to immediate friends and family. "The rest will all come together."

Finally the Bride

They bark with laughter as you sway in a daze of happiness. *This is what it feels like to be so in love. This is what it feels like to finally get engaged.*

STEP THREE: CALL 9-1-1

You have three panic attacks in one day. You wonder if you should call 9-1-1. "I need an ambulance," you proclaim from underneath your bed, where you're sitting with dirty socks, piles of old shoes, and your laptop that's filled with Excel spreadsheets and Pinterest boards. He asks what's wrong. What hurts? What can he do? You don't respond to the questions, because your heart is racing, and you can't seem to catch your breath. He takes the laptop from you, tucks you into bed. Tells you that wedding planning doesn't have to be so stressful.

He explains that you'll figure it all out. Repeats what you say: "It will all come together; it's just details!" You feel your body getting hot, you hear those words echo like lyrics to a Chainsmokers song you just can't shut off. "NO IT WON'T!" you scream before pulling a weighted blanket over your head and calling it a day.

You decide to accept help, you decide to pay attention to the stranger you meet at the nail salon, on a park bench, behind the counter at CVS when they want to share wedding advice. You write it all down. One person tells you planning

13. HOW TO CANCEL YOUR WEDDING

a big wedding is a waste: you should just elope in Italy like they did. Another says you must plan the biggest wedding you can. A third tells you that you should start dieting for your wedding now. You tell them you don't even have a wedding date! They say it's never too early, if you know what they mean. You don't at all know what they mean.

You build a website for people to give their opinions in an organized way. You create options for them to vote on. You make business cards and hand them out whenever people try to plan your wedding for you. "Go to the website," you say. "Share the advice there." You feel in control. You feel on top of the world.

You invite strangers to join in. Before you know it, one million people have voted on your wedding. You let them pick the date, pick the location, pick the theme, pick what kind of entertainment you'll have, you let them pick it all. You don't, ever, feel regret about it. You never have a panic attack again.

Your friends ask you why you think this is a good idea, and you tell them it's not. Good ideas don't make it into the wedding-planning process. It's the only idea. You don't tell them it's the only idea for a person who is indecisive and the definition of a bridezilla. You just tell them you're happy this way. "Don't worry," you say, "it will all come together; it's just details."

Finally the Bride

You get the results. You will have a wedding in October 2020, and it will be in Florida. You exhale a ball of stress. You pick out wedding vendors with enough research and vetting that you'd think you were shopping for a new house. You sign contracts with them and pay them deposits. You have a whole team of people locked into making this October wedding the biggest party of your lifetime.

You tell everyone how excited you are. You tell them it's the wedding you always dreamed of. You do a TV interview and recommend that everyone out there should let strangers plan their wedding too.

You don't let anyone, even your fiancé, know how deeply wrong it all feels, how you get these pings in your gut that something isn't right, that none of this will ever actually come together. You never let it show. You only make people think it's right.

STEP FOUR: INVITE EVERYONE YOU DON'T WANT TO INVITE TO YOUR WEDDING

Invite people to the wedding you have no idea why you're inviting but know you have to invite. These are the people who exist in your life just so you can see them at special occasions. Your mom says if you don't invite Cousin Barbara, then you won't see her for another ten years, and she is a person you're supposed to see every five years. You wonder if everyone has

13. HOW TO CANCEL YOUR WEDDING

family members that only exist to fill the rooms at weddings, bar mitzvahs, and funerals. You wonder why, in this family, nobody sees each other in between.

Finalize your guest list but show it to nobody. If it leaks, you know it will get longer. Tell your aunt Iris that you left the list at home, whoops! Think of an answer when she asks if you've sent an invitation to your second cousin's ex-husband, Dan. Before you have the chance to respond, watch as she texts him the date, time, and location and then texts you his address. Wonder how you never realized your family members have the tenacity of an executive assistant.

Send out your save the dates and wallow in sadness over all the people you didn't invite. Question if you should have just sent a pity invitation to your old boss who likes your LinkedIn posts. Question if you should have invited your neighbor. You adore your neighbor! Why wouldn't you just invite her? Scratch your head in dismay over whether you should have just sent out a handful of invitations to college friends you've had a falling out with. Stress over what will happen if years later you rekindle the friendship, only to regret not having them there at the biggest day of your life.

You address save the dates to all of these people and put them on a shelf in your coat closet. You vow to send these out if the guilt doesn't settle in a week's time.

Finally the Bride

STEP FIVE: REALIZE YOU MIGHT HAVE TO CANCEL THIS WEDDING

Pick at your eyebrow hair as you watch the news and realize this pandemic you thought would go away won't be going away. Feel embarrassed that you just mailed out save the dates and now you're going to have to mail out un-save the dates. Wonder if you can call the post office and get them to stop delivering these pieces of mail. Realize, no, you can't call the post office and get them to stop delivering these pieces of mail. Understand that wedding brain ruffles your logic around in the most mysterious kind of way.

Realize it's June and the wedding is in October. If you don't cancel now, it will get awkward. People will have to muster up the courage to tell you they can't come because of the virus. You don't want people to have to do that. Realize you have to cancel and you have to cancel fast.

Ask your fiancé what he thinks. When he says he thinks you should cancel, yell at him that this is all his fault. Remind him of how you didn't want to get married. Rub it in his face that you wanted to get married but then he wasn't ready. Secretly agree when he says this argument is a waste of time.

Sit together, silently, as you watch the news flash numbers on the screen and realize the world has bigger plans, bigger problems, a bigger pandemic than you ever imagined unfolding before you.

13. HOW TO CANCEL YOUR WEDDING

You know your fiancé feels bad about this. Know you will always feel worse.

STEP SIX: DECIDE TO DO NOTHING

Forget about it all and convince yourself that maybe it will all be okay. Maybe if you don't cancel the wedding, you'll wake up one morning in August and the whole world will be better. *Make it to July*, you tell yourself, then you'll decide.

Get a phone call from friends who say they love you but they don't think they can make it. Get a phone call from a family member who says they already booked their hotel and plans to be there, no matter what.

Get a phone call from the DJ who says he needs to know soon what your reception entrance song will be. He needs you to approve your wedding playlist of dance floor songs.

"Soon? The wedding is months away," you respond with hesitation.

"Soon," he says, without saying that once you do this, you're locked into the contract and can't cancel on him.

"Read the fine print," he says, later on, when you go to ask for your money back: once you pay the deposit and start planning your playlist, you lose your right to cancel.

Blast the song "Everybody Dance Now" on repeat for one hour. You want to get your money's worth.

STEP SEVEN: GOOGLE "HOW TO CANCEL A WEDDING"

Scroll through a roundup of the cutest wedding postponement notices that couples have sent out. Read an article about how to get wedding deposits back. Spend an hour on Reddit reading about how the wedding industry is a billion-dollar scam. Wonder how you knew that to be true but how you suddenly forgot it the second you said the word *yes*.

Sigh at the fact that canceling the wedding might be the best thing that's ever happened to you. Start to exhale in joy over the thought of canceling and how replanning the wedding later on will help you make none of these mistakes ever again. You won't invite Cousin Barbara this time. You won't sign a contract for extra-large bouquets of flowers at a few hundred bucks each.

Worry that yes, you will: yes, you will make all those same mistakes again.

STEP EIGHT: CANCEL THE WEDDING

Draft an email to your wedding vendors. Make it blunt and simple: "We need to cancel the wedding because of the pandemic." Worry that you'll be out $10,000 in cash. Wonder what else you would have done with that money. You could have planned a trip to Europe, rented out that apartment overlooking the bakery you love in the West Village for a few

13. HOW TO CANCEL YOUR WEDDING

months, bought a used convertible. Ask yourself if you want any of that. Realize that you have no idea what you actually want anymore.

Wait as the responses trickle in from your wedding vendors. The DJ says no, you can't get your money back. Ask if you can get back some of it. He agrees to refund half of your deposit, but he says he's keeping the rest. Tell him to keep his lame playlist too. All the other vendors are understanding about it and give your money back, except the vendor that took the most, the actual venue.

They don't answer. You call, you email, you mail a written letter. You never hear back from them.

STEP NINE: INFORM YOUR GUEST LIST

Tell everyone you're over it. Dress yourself with this put together attitude of being completely nonchalant and unphased by this news. Tell your fiancé you don't care how he does it, just erase this wedding from our lives. You treat him like he's your assistant canceling your lunch plans. He finds wedding postponement cards with pink flowers on them. You suddenly get nauseous by the color pink.

You throw his phone at the couch when he shows you. NO, NO, NO! You tell him you'll direct this project now, like you're Anna Wintour, firing him from the job in a sick way that at the same time brings you an unprecedented moment of pure joy.

You decide to do something different. Something bold. Something odd. You create a card that explains the wedding is off, for now, and write, "Love Always Wins. We Hope You Do Too." You add a scratch-off lottery ticket inside each envelope.

You have this weird feeling that Cousin Barbara will be the one who wins the jackpot. *Of course she'll be the one who wins the big prize.*

STEP TEN: PUT AN END TO THIS WEDDING

Watch the news. Watch the news for so long you realize you should have canceled this wedding weeks ago. Walk slowly to the mailbox. Slide each cancelation notice into the slot. There are 170. You put each one in as if you're putting important documents into the shredder. You wait after each one for a response. You don't get one.

You're honest about it. You are waiting for someone to stop you. Wouldn't this be a great time for that Publishers Clearing House guy to show up with balloons and a prize check? You'd donate the money, but still, you're desperate for the attention.

13. HOW TO CANCEL YOUR WEDDING

You drop the last few in the mail. You regret it so badly that you stick your fingers inside the mail slot to try to pull them out.

STEP ELEVEN: CHANGE YOUR MIND 1,000 TIMES
Fall madly in love with a wedding you felt was wrong. Fall madly in love with a venue even though they won't give you your money back. Fall madly in love with each and every name on your guest list, even the people you hardly wanted there.

Fall madly in love with what you no longer have. Laugh at how you're supposed to be happy when other people get what you want. Look around to make sure nobody is watching. You don't want anyone to find out how you really feel. You feel like a character inside the movie *Monsters, Inc.* You pray someone will animate what you should do next.

STEP TWELVE: WAIT TO HEAR FROM PEOPLE—WAIT TO HEAR FROM ANYONE
Weeks go by, and you know people got your wedding cancelation cards, but you don't hear from anyone. Nobody. Okay, sure, you hear from ten people, but those are people you'd hear from anyway. They are your immediate family members and closest friends. They didn't win a penny, but they did get your cancelation card.

Finally the Bride

Wait to hear from anybody else. There are 160 people who haven't reached out, who didn't send an email, haven't picked up the phone. Surely, they will, they will soon. Weeks go by and you don't hear from anyone.

Come on, you think. *Somebody at least had to win.* You think about your early days living in New York City, realizing your salary would never be enough to pay all your bills, sitting in your closet with a pile of scratch-offs, knowing that eventually you'd win.

You start casually reaching out, calling friends, sending text messages.

"Hey, Sandy! What did you think of our wedding cancelation cards?"

Sandy shares that she won $10. You ask Sandy why she didn't mention it, why she didn't reach out.

"I thought, yeah, I guess I thought I should give you space?"

Space? You want to yell at her, but you don't, because what you wanted more than space was for someone to feel sorry for you. You wanted someone to just say they felt sorry for you.

STEP THIRTEEN: VOW TO PLAN NOTHING EVER AGAIN

Confess to people that this wasn't the wedding of your dreams, that you didn't want any of this anyway. Confess to

13. HOW TO CANCEL YOUR WEDDING

other people how heartbroken you are about the cancelation of your October wedding.

Realize that one thing most people who know you don't know about you is that you have the ability to feel two completely different things, strongly and strangely, at the same time.

Find it odd that people who never reached out to express their sadness over the cancelation or exclaim their big lottery wins are the ones asking you what you've got planned next.

Think about replying:

Hey, the first round wasn't good enough for you?

Give up on trying to respond, and say nothing instead.

STEP FOURTEEN: REALIZE YOU NOW HAVE TO CELEBRATE AN EX-WEDDING DAY

Your calendar has a date on it you can't just miss. Forget when your dentist appointment is, sure, but your ex-wedding day? Try and the world will remind you. People ask what you've got planned. People offer suggestions. One person tells you to spend your entire wedding budget on that day. Your brain goes back to that used convertible. Another person tells you to order a pizza and cry your eyes out watching one of those wedding movies that always ends well. You nod your head, hand them a business card to voice their opinions on the

Finally the Bride

website you built, and try to figure out how to forget about an entire day.

For a second you wonder if you should just go buy $10,000 worth of lottery tickets and hope you get lucky. Ha! Who are you kidding? You know you won't get lucky.

Play your wedding entrance song: "Everybody Dance Now."

Play it again. Play it one more time. Realize that the number one thing nobody tells you about wedding planning and canceling a wedding is that none of it makes sense and you doubt every ounce of who you are to the point where you find yourself getting your pinky finger caught inside a mailbox to fetch out your cancelation cards.

Realize that you will be okay. Realize that all of this, in some odd way, was supposed to be messed up because it was a mess anyway.

Realize that even though you are back to square one, maybe you'll plan something better. Maybe you'll make all the same mistakes again.

But you know what you won't ever do? Pick "Everybody Dance Now" as the song you enter your wedding reception to. No. In fact, you will make it a point to never listen to it again.

"You hear that, Siri? Delete 'Everybody Dance Now' and October 17, 2020, from my life."

You smile wide as Siri says, "Deleting now."

13. HOW TO CANCEL YOUR WEDDING

Stand still as your fiancé grabs your hand, like you're slow dancing around the wedding venue in Florida, only you are inside your tiny Brooklyn living room, and listen as he says, "It will all come together."

Grab his hand tighter and understand that he is right. Pick up the pace in the way your feet move when you dance around to silence with the person you're madly in love with on what has now become your ex-wedding day. Feel, truly, madly, deeply, that none of this matters much anyway, the wedding part—only the love part matters.

The rest, you suppose, is just details.

Chapter 14

AND THE SECRET TO MARRIAGE IS . . .

Adam is making eye contact with the moving clouds above, digging his toes into the dewy grass, and thinking hard about his answer to a question he's heard fifteen times before. He's finally agreed to do something unusual and uncomfortable with me. He's finally agreed to go see a marriage therapist.

"I'll only go if . . ." he starts to say, but pauses again to wallow in his thoughts. The yes rolls off his tongue, but his list of demands is a bit slower and calculated. My brain runs full speed around this moment of silence, and I wonder what he will ask for.

Perhaps he will say . . .

I'll only go if you stop asking me to do these weird pre-wedding challenges.

We've been engaged for a year, and in that time, I've dragged Adam to see a divorce lawyer and a financial expert. I can see why he's mentally exhausted tagging along with my

14. AND THE SECRET TO MARRIAGE IS...

agenda to try to understand all the gobbledygook around getting married and what it actually all means.

I'll only go if you don't tell anyone.

I start to wonder if Adam is over me sharing every bit of our relationship and engagement with the world. I wouldn't blame him. Millions of people have been voting on our wedding decisions, and he's hardly complained about it. Maybe it's all been bottling up, and us seeing a marriage therapist just isn't something he wants the public to know about.

I'll only go if you promise to listen to what the marriage therapist says.

I bet he's going to say this, and even though seeing a marriage therapist is something I really want to do, I don't think I can agree to this. I'm a stubborn Aries, Enneagram number four, type A human who likes to be in control and who has issues listening to anyone's advice.

Plus, I'm not eager to see the marriage therapist because Adam and I have relationship problems we need an expert to help us solve. I'm going out of fear that everything will change once we say "I do" on our wedding day, and if that's going to happen, I want to know about it in advance.

I got the idea to do this after a few people told me how everything changes once you get married.

My friend Samantha once told me how she'd lie to everyone who asked her if marriage changes anything. She didn't want to be the only one who was honest in saying that after the wedding ends, the disappointment of having nothing to look forward to really starts to rattle the relationship.

"What do you mean 'be the only one'?" I asked her, wondering if all the married couples I know are in cahoots together and lying about being so happy and in love.

"I just don't think people are so forthcoming about how reality settles in after the wedding and the relationship gets stale, fast."

Another friend, Sheila, constantly tells me that marriage makes you argue with your partner 75% more than when you were just dating. She's data obsessed and tracks their fights on an Excel spreadsheet.

"I have proof!" she says, showing me the rise of disagreements and tiffs that happened right after they tied the knot.

I met a stranger in the supermarket who saw I was engaged and told me to put off getting married for as long as possible.

"Why?" I asked, awkwardly squeezing avocados, waiting for her tidbit of information.

"Being engaged is the peak of your relationship roller coaster," she explained, taking her hand and lifting it up to the sky. "But honey, what comes up . . ."

I dropped the avocados and finished her sentence.

"Must go down."

14. AND THE SECRET TO MARRIAGE IS . . .

Some friends have told me the opposite: that if you've been with your partner for a while, getting married just feels like the "same old, same old."

"But doesn't *old* imply boring?" I asked my friend Madline one afternoon.

"Only if you're expecting your relationship to always feel magical. It's not Disney World fun. Marriage is more like your neighborhood playground with one old slide."

All of this made me wonder if speaking to a marriage therapist would give Adam and I the heads-up on how we ignore all the things people have told us and instead pursue a happy, consistent, and healthy relationship.

Plus, speaking to a marriage therapist would nicely round out the tips we got from the divorce lawyer (who told us what changes when people get married legally) and the financial expert (who helped us understand how to merge and separate our finances).

When I first brought this up to Adam, he immediately said, "No way," before I could even finish the phrase "marriage therapist."

"Come on, Jen," he responded. "We've already talked to a divorce lawyer. Why this?"

"I just don't want our relationship to feel like the plunge of a roller coaster, like the final drop of Splash Mountain."

"Huh?"

I didn't even bother telling him about my interaction with the woman at the supermarket. I just dropped the topic and brought it up two days later instead.

"So I figure if we see a marriage therapist . . ."

Adam's eyebrows curved up, and he shook his head.

I waited another two days.

"Okay, so I found this marriage therapist."

"Jen, we're not even married."

"But soon we will be, and right now we're at the peak of our roller coaster."

"I seriously don't understand this roller coaster stuff."

I waited another two days. This went on for an entire month until, finally, I made progress.

"Marriage therapist?" is all I have to say the day Adam finally agrees.

"I'll go if she can tell us the secret to a happy and long-lasting marriage."

I go over and give Adam a hug. I love that his ultimatum for going involves learning the secret to this whole marriage thing because it shows, for the hundredth time during this engagement, that Adam just wants the best for our relationship, whereas I just want everything to be one giant experiment.

We met with Dr. Lisa Marie Bobby, a marriage therapist with fifteen years of experience, over Zoom. We didn't come

14. AND THE SECRET TO MARRIAGE IS . . .

prepared with too many questions. We just asked her to share the things all couples should spend more time working on to improve their relationship.

Here's exactly what she said and how we digested this advice.

- **Psychological flexibility is extremely important.**

One of the first tips Dr. Bobby gave Adam and I really hit home. Wedding planning during COVID-19 was overwhelmingly stressful, and there was so much uncertainty. Figuring out how to not only process that but work together as a couple to make decisions caused a lot of extra arguments and disagreements.

Dr. Bobby shared that getting good at psychological flexibility, which refers to the ability to be able to shift gears, stay in the present, and remain aligned to your most deeply held values—even under stress—is important in a solid relationship.

"This allows you to regulate your own emotions, communicate effectively, and work with your partner to find productive solutions to inevitable problems. When couples can do this together, they're able to stay aligned through thick and thin," said Dr. Bobby.

To get better at this, Adam and I decided to take time, more often, to do meditation and solo check-ins. That way we can stay in control of how we feel and be able to approach pop-up problems and challenges with more clarity, individually, and then together as a couple.

- **Treat each other with kindness.**

When you've been with your partner for quite a while, it can feel easy to forget to do something nice for them quite often. While Adam and I try to make a conscious effort to treat each other to special gifts or kind gestures, it can be easy to forget to do that.

Dr. Bobby shared with us that making an effort to be kind and generous allows a couple to continue to reap the rewards of a loving and enduring partnership.

"How does your partner feel most loved and appreciated by you? Find out, and lavish them with it every chance you can," said Dr. Bobby.

One thing neither Adam nor I ever did was take a free love language test. After we did that, we were able to see how each other likes to receive love. Knowing this will allow us to be more intentional and specific with how we show kindness to the other person.

- **Learn how to have courageous conversations.**

Adam and I speak to each other, what feels like, every second of the day. But one thing we don't do often is dive into tough

14. AND THE SECRET TO MARRIAGE IS . . .

conversions or talk deeply about things that might be awkward or scary to bring up.

Dr. Bobby calls these courageous conversations and believes having more of these helps couples who grow together bravely face the tough stuff authentically and respectfully.

"During courageous conversations, couples share their true thoughts, feelings, needs, and desires with each other and trust that they'll achieve understanding and a deeper union. Couples who avoid courageous conversations will inevitably grow apart," said Dr. Bobby.

Figuring out how to have more of these conversations wasn't the easiest, but we were eager to implement this in our lives. We tried scheduling time once a week to give one another space to open up about anything they were thinking or feeling. Having this scheduled time has allowed us to feel like we can pause from our busy lives and give time to any mini-struggles or feelings of tension that we're feeling.

- **Create emotional safety.**

When Adam and I started to think about the key elements of a solid relationship, we wondered if good communication was everything. While it's important, Dr. Bobby said that having emotional safety is a primary, foundational component of a healthy relationship.

Finally the Bride

"It needs to be okay for both partners to not be okay sometimes," said Dr. Bobby. "Emotional safety is created when both people are able to manage their reactivity, anger, and judgment in order to remain compassionately present with each other's needs for a soft place to fall . . . apart. Couples who understand how to truly be there for each other, without 'fixing,' advice-giving, avoiding, or criticism will deepen their connection—not despite the rough patches of life, but because of them."

To get better at this, Adam and I went through an activity of writing down phrases we can say to each other when we don't feel like we're giving one another the safety to open up and express ourselves. This is something that we feel we're decent at but can always improve upon.

- **Respect the system.**

One big takeaway we had after speaking to Dr. Bobby was that being in a relationship and getting married is so much more than two separate individuals existing together; it's about working together.

"This means that people are not just existing independently. They are reacting and responding to each other's reactions, ad infinitum. By understanding that your partner's reactions are—at least in part—influenced by what you are putting into the system, you immediately become empowered to

14. AND THE SECRET TO MARRIAGE IS . . .

change it," said Dr. Bobby. "Not by demanding change in your partner, but rather by getting extremely deliberate about what you are contributing to the system and how that's impacting your partner."

This is something I know we can struggle with especially during difficult or stressful times, like planning a wedding. Remembering that we're a team, we're partners, we're in this together, makes it easier to view relationship development as a priority.

Finally, before we ended the call with Dr. Bobby, we asked her the question that meant the most to Adam:

"What is the secret to a long-lasting and happy marriage?"

I grabbed my pen and scribbled her answer on a napkin, almost desperate to consume her advice, as if it were a love potion or a magical spell. For a person like me who is usually so reluctant to listen to anyone's advice, I felt a sudden pull to take her tips seriously and embrace them. She's not only an expert, but she has worked with thousands of couples over the last fifteen years at all stages in their relationship.

What scares me the most about marriage is the unknown, the what-ifs, the number of relationships that simply fail. But perhaps sulking in the words of Dr. Bobby and taking her secret to a happy marriage seriously is just what I need to ease into such a big next step in life.

"The secret to a long-lasting relationship is learning to challenge each other, growing individually, and never forgetting to focus on those little moments."

Later, I ask Adam why it was so important to ask that question to Dr. Bobby.

"Because I wanted you to hear it from someone else."

"Hear what?"

"That all this marriage stuff isn't about how much changes. Maybe it's just about how much we believe in us and all we already do to make our relationship great?"

"Did you know that what she said would be the secret?"

"No! But I did know it wasn't going to be something negative and scary. I knew it was going to be what we already knew."

After meeting with so many experts, I'm starting to believe that Adam is right. Marriage isn't just what everyone tries to tell you it's going to be. Every expert out there will have a different version of stuff you need to know and need to do, and perhaps it's good to check in with them, but in the end, there's no real 100% foolproof secret.

Every couple is different, and what makes one couple make it and another couple not make it is one million tiny, little things that would take forever to learn. We don't have that much time, and plus, I'm no good at tracking things on Excel like Sheila.

14. AND THE SECRET TO MARRIAGE IS . . .

So I guess I truly believe that the real secret to a long-lasting marriage is for both people to try to continue to work on themselves, work with each other, and remember it all just takes work.

That's just another day as a human being, and some days we're superstars at doing it, and other days we're a mess.

So maybe the secret is forgiveness or understanding?

Maybe the secret is learning to be nice to ourselves and each other?

Ah! I bet the true secret is always having pizza in the freezer as a pick-me-up for the other person.

Or maybe there's just no secret at all?

Yeah, I guess the secret is, there's just no secret at all.

And I love that. I really love that.

Chapter 15
THE SADDEST BRIDE I EVER DID SEE

The saddest bride I ever did see was the missing bride I found, after the ceremony ended, French kissing the carpet inside her bridal suite.

Or at least that's what it looked like.

"Um, Juliana?" I slowly whispered to the bride as I eyed her, face down, sprawled out in her poofy white dress, swirling her tongue in patterns on the floor. "What's wrong?"

She closed her mouth and tilted her head sideways, leaving one eye open and the other smushed on the ground.

I tossed the bouquet over my left shoulder and ran over to her.

"Are you okay?"

She didn't answer, but the closer I got, the more I was able to piece together what was really going on.

To her left, a shattered bottle of vodka and giant pieces of glass sat on the floor, holding remnants of liquid like miniature life rafts.

15. THE SADDEST BRIDE I EVER DID SEE

Juliana picked up each glass shard one by one and slurped the vodka off it like she was indulging in all-you-can-eat oysters at a Vegas buffet.

"Juliana!" I yelled, pulling the glass out of her hands.

She was drunk. Blasted! The ceremony had ended only thirty minutes ago, and she'd been hiding here, sneaking in some alone time with her secret significant other. Vodka.

She sat up and noticed the glass everywhere, quickly opening her mouth to either speak or puke, puke or speak.

If she did puke, it wouldn't have been the first time a bride had hurled all over me.

Handling bodily fluids should make its way to the tippy top of my job description. People think my job as a professional bridesmaid is filled with glitz and glamour, but what it's filled with are so many *P* words—puke, pee, and dare I even say it, poop. When you work up close and personal with people on a big day of their lives, you get hit with everything.

I had a bride puke on my bridesmaid dress five minutes before walking down the aisle, another on the morning of her wedding because she was too hungover to get out of bed, and another when I went to say goodbye at the end of the night: she greeted me with a drunk burst of puke that flew out of her mouth like confetti leaving a party popper.

When Juliana opened her mouth, to my surprise, it wasn't what I expected. It wasn't liquid and it wasn't a coherent sentence. It was just a loud, piercing scream—the kind you finally let out after feeling so disappointed and frustrated, hopeless and exhausted.

Sort of like when you are digging for that one bag of chips in the pantry, and all of a sudden, an entire shelf gets unhinged and everything falls on your toe. It was exactly the kind of sound you make when everything falls on your toe.

"AHHHHHHHHHH!" Juliana let it out again, reaching around the carpet for more shattered glass to lick.

That's when the saddest bride I ever did see said the saddest line I ever did hear at any wedding, ever.

"This is the worst day of my life!"

Six years later, when I wake up at 3 am and can't go back to sleep because my mind is montaging the moments of my life so far, this is usually the third or fourth thing I think about.

"This is the worst day of my life!"

I took ten steps back, moving closer and closer toward the exit door. I had only been working weddings for a couple of months at that point, and I wasn't prepared for any of this. I thought about running. I flirted with quitting.

But the saddest brides are the most thrilling, and so I stayed.

"I think I need to go find the groom," I started to say. But as my hand turned the doorknob left, someone else's turned it right.

15. THE SADDEST BRIDE I EVER DID SEE

In walked Juliana's mom, aunt, and cousin. Juliana fell backward onto the carpet, her fingers feeling around for a puddle of vodka.

"Everything is fine! I know it doesn't look that way, but it is that way!" I announced in my most professional tone of voice, quickly interrupted by Juliana.

"AHHHH."

"Is this really happening? Right now, Juliana? Really?" her mom said.

"Come on, I knew it. Didn't you see it coming?" her aunt said.

"This is so embarrassing," her cousin said.

I heard a rumble in the hallway, and I knew it had to be the groom. *Let him see this,* I thought. *Let him see this and save this.*

A part of me wanted to pat him on the back and wish him a warm welcome into marriage, ask if it was everything he expected, and question him over why he didn't come find Juliana sooner. But there wasn't time. Instead, I put my hand on his back and used the force of my biceps to push him inside the room.

Inside, Juliana was no longer flat on the ground. Juliana was on her hands and knees, banging on the floor like she was a two-year-old having a temper tantrum inside a Target.

Finally the Bride

The saddest brides are also so mesmerizing.

The groom stood behind me as if to use the professional bridesmaid as a shield.

"Do something, okay?" I shoved him forward once more. "Just do something."

He didn't do anything. Nobody did. We all just watched Juliana and her arms, like drumsticks, beating on the ground.

"Everyone get out," I screamed. "Everyone! Out!"

Nobody knew that I wasn't a professional, that I had just started the business only a few months ago after my Craigslist ad had taken off. I'd had absolutely zero experience with sad brides, only happy ones, so far. I'd dealt with happy tears, happy smiles, happy hugs hello and goodbye. Not anymore. Juliana showed me a side of weddings I did not know existed. The side they don't show you in movies. The side they try to show you in reality shows, but you write it off as being scripted and fake. A side you hope you never see again, though a part of you deep down to the tip of your esophagus knows you will.

The price on my website works for happy brides, brides that ask me to help them go dress shopping and dance to Bruno Mars. Brides that make me wear chiffon dresses and get their little cousin Sarah to smile in the photos. Happy brides are easy brides. Sad brides are loss leaders.

15. THE SADDEST BRIDE I EVER DID SEE

Nobody listened when I screamed. Everyone was standing still as if they were trapped in a snow globe and Juliana was the one shaking it.

Finally, she took matters into her own hands and tossed an empty champagne flute at the wall. More glass shattered everywhere, and for a moment, as the light caught Juliana's reflection and bounced off the tiny pieces, I noticed how beautiful she looked. Sad brides are just as beautiful as happy brides.

Juliana's mom, her aunt, and her cousin marched out the door in a single file line. I shut it hard and noticed something was missing. Something was gone.

"Where did he go?" I whispered to myself, checking underneath the love seat for the groom. "You have to be kidding me!"

At some point, as the glass hit the wall and pieces flew everywhere, the groom had escaped. He just completely left.

Juliana let me hug her and feed her water from a paper cup. No more glass.

Her words were slurred, but if you listened carefully and didn't interrupt, you were able to understand what she was trying to say.

Juliana confessed just how wrong everything about the day had been, how this wedding was her nightmare and she

Finally the Bride

had never wanted any of this, not the princess dress or high-heeled shoes, not the people on the guest list or the prime rib.

She did not say it out loud, but she forcefully tried to peel the ring off her finger, and I knew she desperately wanted to add the groom to that list.

"I did this all for them, my stupid family. I am miserable!"

We sat in the locked bridal suite for the rest of the cocktail hour and then for another thirty minutes. Nobody came looking for us or cared that we were missing. Juliana was supposed to be one of the main characters of this wedding, but she felt invisible.

When she finally emerged, she looked like she had just run through a lawn sprinkler that shot vodka out of it. The way her mascara tears stained her face looked like she had put on a few tiny temporary tattoos.

Nobody cared when she entered the party. Nobody asked where she had been. Her mom, her aunt, her cousin, and the groom acted like nothing had happened.

On the way home that night, I sat in the back of an old taxi cab, picking slivers of glass out of the bottom of my shoe, crying harder and harder as we traveled south on Fifth Avenue.

"Okay, what is wrong?" the taxi driver forced himself to ask. When the crying is louder than the radio blaring, a person feels obligated to ask.

15. THE SADDEST BRIDE I EVER DID SEE

"I just thought . . . I just thought weddings were supposed to be happy! So freaking happy!"

I blew my nose in my bridesmaid dress.

"But they are sad. Brides are so, so, so, so sad."

"Hey!" he cut me off. "Life is sad, lady. Life is sad."

He cranked the radio up so the volume was almost deafening, which was appreciated because the crying wouldn't stop. I cried so loud you would have thought everything in the entirety of New York City just fell on my toes.

When I got home, I flattened out on the floor and stared at the ceiling, wondering why, for so long, we have all been made to believe that weddings are the best day of a person's life. People tell you that and you believe them. People lie.

"Not me!" I yelled inside an empty room. "I will not be sad."

Yet there I was, almost six years to the day later, looking at my reflection in a large piece of glass, thinking, *The saddest bride I ever did see turned out to be me.*

Chapter 16

A MILLION MORE TOMORROWS

"Please don't tell anyone," I whispered into the phone from the cold tiled floor of my bathroom. "But I'm not sure I want to do this."

The voice on the other end gargled with phlegm or disappointment. I wasn't sure which, but she didn't immediately say anything, which was perfect. It was the only response I wanted to hear anyway.

Finally, she spoke.

"Is this cold feet?" Chelsea asked.

I grabbed my toes and wiggled each one as if they were directly connected to the answers hiding in my heart.

"How would I know if it is cold feet?" I asked.

"Ha, you're asking me? I'm, like, the worst person to ask."

"You're the only person," I replied.

Chelsea was the only number I planned to dial about this. I didn't think about calling Lucie or Claire. I knew I couldn't call Hannah or Brie, unless I wanted the entire Brooklyn dog park to be whispering about my wedding jitters. Yet those

16. A MILLION MORE TOMORROWS

were the friends I considered my best friends, the ones who would have been my bridesmaids if I was having bridesmaids.

Chelsea didn't make that list. She didn't even make the wedding guest list. Honestly, she didn't make any list in my life. Not the Christmas card list or the *I'm in town, want to grab a drink* list. Chelsea wasn't even technically a friend. She was a stranger, once a bride herself who had hired me to help her end her engagement.

When Chelsea first reached out, she said she wanted me as her one and only bridesmaid because her friends were ditzy and dramatic. I perked up at the thought of working with her because she described her wedding as intimate and casual. The gig seemed easy, and the pay was enough to cover my rent for the month. Once she signed the contract and paid the deposit, we met for tea in the center of Manhattan.

"Tell me everything!" I asked, sipping my ginger tea marmalade splash. "What color dress should I wear, and what's the mother-in-law like?"

Chelsea rolled her eyes and shoved the questions away like scone crumbs on the table.

"I lied to get you here today."

I looked around for the emergency exit. I wondered if any of those undercover New York City cops just happened to be lingering around this side-street tea shop at 3 pm on

Finally the Bride

a Sunday. I tried to give the barista panicked eyes, but she pretended to be busy.

"Okay," I replied, digging into my tote for any sharp objects. "And what exactly did you lie about?"

You would think three years into my career as a hired bridesmaid I would have gotten better at background checking these people. You'd think I'd ask for their driver's license or birth certificate or any document to prove they were in fact real and really getting married. But I had recently been laid off from my full-time job and was trying to make enough money to cover my own basics and precious image. The world thought I was a successful, ground-breaking entrepreneur. But really, I was just a single, sad, lonely girl sleeping in the living room of an apartment on Thirty-First Street begging my landlord to give me just a few more days to pay my rent.

So when Chelsea reached out with an email subject that said, "Help, I'm desperate," I took her money and started working with her instantly, no Google search, no last name shared. To be honest, I didn't know where she was getting married or if she was actually getting married.

"I lied about why I hired you."

"You lied about why you hired me?" I repeated, loud enough in hopes that the guy with monster-sized headphones playing Dungeons and Dragons on his 20-inch monitor at

16. A MILLION MORE TOMORROWS

the table next to us would press pause and whisk me away if Chelsea tried to pull something crazy like . . . well, I didn't actually know. I mean, how crazy could a person be if they drank chamomile tea at 3 pm on a Sunday?

"Please don't tell anyone this," she started to say.

I surveyed my surroundings. Even if I wanted to tell someone, nobody in this chic, calm tea shop would care to listen! The guy next to me was still playing his video game. The undercover cops were stuffing mini blueberry bundt cakes into their mouths. The barista still refused to show me both eyes.

"Okay," I calmly replied, giving into my own destiny.

"But I'm not sure I want to do this."

I exhaled. "Oh, this. This! No problem. Hiring a bridesmaid can feel odd. I get it."

I thought about her check sitting in my bank account. How welcome it was there and how empty it would be when I gave her back the deposit. If she was having cold feet about hiring a bridesmaid, I wasn't going to force her to do it.

"No, no," she replied quickly. "It's not you. It's me."

She lifted her hand to show me her ring. It was so big and shiny that the video game guy caught a sliver of the light in his pupil, rubbed his eye, and went back to slaying dragons.

"I'm not sure I want to marry my fiancé anymore."

"Do you have cold feet?" I asked.

Finally the Bride

I could hardly convince a guy to see me for a second date. What did I know about having second thoughts about marrying someone and spending the rest of your life with them? Absolutely nothing.

As I thought about what to say next, Chelsea crossed her leg over her knee and reached for each of her toes dangling off the edge of her sandal. She felt each one as if she was longing for some sort of answer that would travel down her body.

"I don't know," she said.

"Why me?" I asked. "Why did you hire me, lie to me, and get me hopped up on a ginger tea nonalcoholic cocktail to tell me this?"

"Because I have nobody else."

I looked into her gloomy acorn-shaped eyes.

"I have a lot of people, but nobody I can be honest with about this. You don't know me, you probably won't judge me, and after today, we'll probably never see each other again."

Chelsea and I talked for three entire hours. I tried everything an unbiased stranger would do to help diagnose if she was feeling cold feet or completely not in love with this guy.

I asked her one final question. "Do you want to spend five hundred more tomorrows with him?"

"I can't say yes to that," she replied.

"Let's try with fifty. How about fifty?"

"Can we start a little smaller?"

16. A MILLION MORE TOMORROWS

"Five?"

She never actually agreed to five, which I think was enough for her to realize the person she had once agreed to marry was not the person she wanted to marry at all.

By the time we both drained our teacups, it was clear she was going to call off the wedding. She would have no need for a hired bridesmaid but told me I could keep the $1,500 deposit as a thank-you for helping her not ruin her life. I refunded every penny of it and mailed her a box of chamomile tea to drink on lonely Sunday afternoons.

I had no business befriending Chelsea after that. Yet I did. Well, sort of. We never saw each other again, but every so often, I'd text her, or she'd text me, and we'd joke about how cold our feet were even though there was such warmth in our hearts.

So when I found myself, the night before my own wedding, quietly shedding tears on the bathroom floor, she was the only person I wanted to call.

"I haven't actually heard your voice since 2016," she said when she answered.

"You've only technically heard my voice once for three hours," I clarified, and we laughed.

I told Chelsea everything, starting with how a psychic told me I wouldn't find love, then I found it. How stressful it felt being engaged, how COVID canceled the wedding I didn't really want, and how I was planning to get married tomorrow on the sidewalk, without any of my loved ones there.

"I'm supposed to be excited and happy, right?"

"Right," she confirmed.

"Then why do I feel sick to my stomach?"

I didn't want Chelsea to say anything. I didn't need her advice or words of affirmation. I didn't need her to tell me that how I was feeling was normal. I didn't need anything except someone who could listen without judgement.

"I know I'm supposed to be some wedding and love expert," I blabbed on, "but I don't know anything about this stuff when it comes to my own life."

Our call went on so long I started getting pins and needles in my legs from sitting on them on the bathroom floor.

"Do I owe you fifteen hundred dollars for this?" I asked jokingly.

"Call us even," she said back. "But answer this. Do you want to spend a thousand tomorrows with this guy?"

I grabbed my cold bare toes and pulled them one by one until the one and only answer floated down from my brain.

"Honestly?"

"Honestly," she replied.

"Yes, more," I said back. "Millions more."

Chapter 17

SILLY LITTLE DATE

Two weeks before Adam and I decided to get married, I woke up soaked in my own sweat from a dream I'd had about a wedding.

My wedding. Finally! It had come to me. My dream wedding.

"I had a vision," I told Adam in the morning, "of how I want our wedding to actually look."

"I really can't wait to hear this," he said. Ever since he'd known me, whenever anyone in the news or in my life asked me about what kind of wedding I wanted, I'd brush off the question instead of telling them the truth: I didn't know.

Or was it that I didn't really care?

Planning a big, gigantic wedding—with blooming floral arrangements, a caterer suggesting we serve passed caviar-topped canapés during cocktail hour, the long white dress I'd inevitably stain the second it draped my body, and the awkward first dance song that would play behind Adam and I as we bobbed our shoulders and swung our toes around like

Finally the Bride

stuffed paper dolls—never seemed appetizing to me. It wasn't something I craved.

Deep within me, I'd always known I didn't want a wedding. But it took a whole lot of drama and lies to get that to come to the surface.

When I was little, I would spend hours playing with Barbies, pretending they all married each other. Every afternoon, a new wedding happened, and I planned the whole thing. I picked the outfits, assigned which dolls were the vendors, and picked the two lucky ones who would walk down the aisle that day.

I understood weddings from TV shows and books. But the whole elaborate celebration seemed empty because it was pretend. The most important part was always missing: the love.

At middle school sleepover parties, we'd each take turns sharing what we wanted our weddings to look like when we got older.

"Big, big roses everywhere!"

"A veil that a queen would wear!"

"I just want to look as beautiful as a Disney princess."

17. SILLY LITTLE DATE

The girls would go on and on, and I'd sit there quietly, taking notes inside my head. They wanted all of these things that I never did. Was there something wrong with me?

"Okay, Jen," one of them would always ask after everyone else spoke first, "your turn."

I never had any idea what to say. I had dreams. I dreamt of reading every book in the library by the time I was thirty. I dreamt of writing books that would be in the library by that time too. Occasionally, I dreamt of falling in love with a guy who made me bounce around with cartoon-like hearts above my head. But never, not even once, did I dream about my own wedding.

"I guess . . . I hope . . ." I had to think fast and pull out some sort of lie. "Well, everything you all said! I want that too!"

Giggles would fly, and all the girls would crawl a little closer until one would say, "May we all grow up and have our dream weddings come true!" And we'd cheers our Ring Pops and fall asleep the second the sugar turned to dust.

When you don't know what you want, sometimes you end up doing exactly what you don't want instead. Or worse, what other people want.

Finally the Bride

After Adam and I got engaged, I pretended we were Barbie dolls. I asked myself what the middle school girls at the sleepover would want for their wedding. When that wasn't enough to suppress the looming doom, I turned to the internet.

"Dear world," I posted, "I'm finally going to be the bride. Plan my wedding for me!"

If that doesn't scream, "She doesn't want a wedding!" I'm not sure what does.

Months after getting engaged, I found myself in the back office of a wedding venue in Delray Beach, Florida, with a check for $5,000 in my hand.

"Sign here and it's official," the venue director said, plucking the check out of my hands.

"Official," I lightly and quietly gagged.

The entire wedding day played out in my mind. Guests showing up in chunky heels and polyester-lined dresses. A DJ playing Bruno Mars and a photographer begging me to smile with every organ in my body.

"Wait, I don't want to do this!" I wish I had said, grabbing my money out of his hands and running away from someone else's wedding dreams at that darling little south Florida venue.

17. SILLY LITTLE DATE

But instead, I took the ballpoint pen out of his hand and signed a contract that said I'd hand over a large chunk of savings in exchange for a wedding I didn't actually want.

I've never been good at standing up for myself or expressing what I really want. I've carried on dwindled relationships in the hopes that they'd break up with me first so I didn't have to do it.

That's what happened with this wedding. It broke up with me first, *thank God.*

With good intentions, we mailed out our save the dates on March 5th, 2020, for a wedding on October 17th, 2020. Soon after, ambulance sirens haunted New York City. COVID had come to town, and it wasn't in a rush to leave.

The idea of getting married in 2020 evaporated as if I had hired a magician to make the entire thing go away.

As quickly as we sent out wedding save the dates, we sent out wedding cancellation notices, which brought in text messages from the people who loved us dearly.

"We're so sorry you're canceling the wedding."

"We know it will be back on soon."

"You must be devastated! How are you feeling?"

I didn't want to be honest with any of them, but if I was, I would have said, "I'm so relieved. Sad, yes, but relieved."

I'm feeling free, I said in my head. "I'm feeling blah," I said instead.

"What if," I began, slowly sharing my vision for our wedding five months after the one we had originally planned.

"What if what?" Adam asked back.

"What if we threw it all away?"

"Go on."

"In my wedding dream, it hit me. There's only one special thing that matters to me about our wedding."

"Again, I can't wait to hear what that is."

"Aside from marrying you, of course," I clarified. "The only thing that matters is that we get married at the place we met, the minute we met, on the day that we met."

I grabbed my phone and sat down beside him, pressing down on the calendar icon.

"Look at this!" I counted the days. "In ten days from now, it'll be the fifth anniversary of our first date at the coffee shop."

"You want to get married at a coffee shop on March nineteenth? That's your dream wedding?"

"No! Well, yes. But I want to get married at the coffee shop THIS March nineteenth."

New York City was still a mess. People were still covering their faces with fabric masks, and giant-sized hand sanitiz-

17. SILLY LITTLE DATE

ers were on every single counter. Our calendars were filled with Zoom calls: a cocktail-making class with friends from summer camp, a catch-up with friends from kindergarten we hadn't spoken to since.

Adam sat still with the idea while I carried on.

"I know it's soon, but who cares? I never wanted any of this wedding stuff, never, not once in my entire life. I want this! I want to marry you at that coffee shop, and I want to do it in ten days because why wait any longer? COVID might last forever, and I desperately need to move on from people asking me about my vision of a dream wedding."

Adam thought about it for a little bit, and finally *he said yes.*

Days before March 19th, 2021, I called in a few favors. I asked my friend Susan Shek, an incredible photographer I met working at a wedding in 2015, if she would come take our photos. *She said yes.*

I called Irving Farm Coffee, the scene of our first date, and asked if we could get married there. *They said no.*

"It's COVID," they said.

"I understand, but what if we wear masks?"

"We're open for business that day: we can't have disruptions."

March is a foolishly chilly month in New York City. But I was desperate for a yes.

"Can we do it outside?"

Finally the Bride

Finally, they said yes.

We asked our parents and a few close loved ones if they'd watch live on Zoom.

Some of them asked why we were doing it this way. Some of them were crushed that they couldn't be there in person. *Eventually, all said yes.*

We asked a few local New York City friends if they wanted to come in person. *A few said yes.* One of my closest friends, Tracy, offered to bake pastries.

We asked Adam's brother to marry us. *He said yes.*

We rushed to J.Crew for a suit for Adam. I bought one for Goofy (the dog) on Amazon. I looked in every store on Broadway in SoHo for a dress that felt right, but I found nothing. I came across a gold sequined suit online and paid fifty-six dollars in rush shipping fees to have it arrive the very next day. It was perfect.

I called the florist down the block and asked if she could make me a bouquet. "A bride should have one!" she declared with passion after learning my wedding plans. She dropped off the most beautiful bouquet, which I accidentally forgot to bring with me on the actual wedding day.

That was it.

Adam and I got married on March 19th, 2021, at around 12:30pm, at the same time, at the same place, on the same date as we'd met five years earlier.

17. SILLY LITTLE DATE

It turns out, all I ever cared about for my dream wedding was simple: marrying the right person on a date that had meaning.

It took me so long to write this chapter because it felt silly to admit that a date had such powerful meaning that it caused me to make a decision where we had a sidewalk street wedding isolated from most of the people we love, including our parents. It wasn't an easy decision to make. The night before the wedding, I really did almost call the whole thing off because I felt such pains of guilt about what we'd decided to do and how we hadn't waited for the day we could do it with our parents by our side.

Even on the morning of the wedding, my chest tightened over who we were letting down by doing what we felt was the only thing we wanted to do: get married on March 19th, that March 19th, and not wait for the next one or two to pass.

So we did it. We said, "I do," as people swung the coffee shop's front door open and shut to order their hot lattes. Our friends looked on, and our family did too, over Zoom. It was quick and lasted just a few minutes. But after Adam stomped on the glass (a Jewish wedding tradition) and we kissed, I looked up at the sky and thought about how silly our dreams are when we finally claim them, own them, admit them out loud.

Finally the Bride

We planned to celebrate March 19th the same way every year for as long as we could by going to that little coffee shop and ordering the exact drinks we had on our first date.

But two years later, on March 19th, 2023, something else happened.

Already two weeks past my due date, after enjoying an anniversary chai latte at Irving Farm Coffee, sidewalk stepping miles all over New York City to get the baby out, and ignoring calls from my doctor about getting induced, at 8:03 pm, on March 19th, 2023, I went into labor with Gemma LoveJoy.

Now, it would be quite the tearjerker to say that she was born on March 19th, 2023, but my stubborn Aries came out forty hours later, on March 21st.

Even so, at 8:03 pm, when I felt a contraction for the very first time, I felt my stomach, looked at Adam, and thought, *This silly little date. It truly is some kind of magic.*

Chapter 18

FINALLY THE BRIDE

A reporter from *The New York Times* called to interview me a day before the wedding. Her first question an obvious one: "After being a bridesmaid for so many strangers, how does it feel to finally be the bride?"

My wedding was about to make headlines all over the place, from *People* magazine to *The Washington Post*. I could see it now, the article running with the title in big bold letters. The news loves a story that feels like a real-life rom-com: *Always a Bridesmaid Finally Becomes the Bride.*

Finally? That sounded like it took me 127 years to find someone to love me. As if they had contacted Diane the psychic before calling me to hear her thoughts on the whole ordeal and all she could say was, "I have no idea how that one finally found love."

Finally makes it sound like I crossed the finish line of a marathon I'd trained for for years. And sure, I went on a bunch of dates and sought out the advice of a really bad psychic,

Finally the Bride

but getting married never felt like the grand accomplishment everyone made it seem like.

I've never gotten so many likes on one Facebook post as I did when I shared that I was engaged—not when I graduated college, started a business, or published a book.

All of those things were harder than getting married. None of those things matter to our culture or society as much as getting married does. Why is that? Why do people not celebrate finally being single! Finally having the courage to ask your boss for a raise you deserve. Finally going to therapy—oomph, they should hand out free coffee mugs for that one.

"It felt like an impossible circumstance to find love, and it did happen. I feel lucky," I responded. "But I don't feel it deserves any kind of award of merit."

"So you two got married and ended up in this thing?" the cashier at 7-Eleven asked, ringing us up for a pile of *New York Times* the day the story ran. "How did you end up in the newspaper? Are you one of those movie stars?"

"Everyone seemed amazed that I finally got married. Don't most people get married? I guess I was always labeled the bridesmaid and people were shocked . . ."

18. FINALLY THE BRIDE

Thankfully, he cut me off before I could finish.

"I've been married forty-six years," he said, tapping his ring finger on the glass counter. "And my biggest piece of advice is, just because you're finally married doesn't mean any of this will be easy or breezy. So good luck, and maybe they'll write about you again if you make it to forty-six."

"That's the real accomplishment," I agreed.

"The wedding doesn't mean a thing."

"Tell me about it." My eyes rolled.

With a stack of newspapers in my arms, I felt this whole wedding thing wouldn't be over until I made a few things clear.

"Finally," I texted Chelsea.

"FINALLY!!!!" I emailed the psychic Diane.

I grabbed a Sharpie from my purse and flipped open the newspaper. I crossed out the word *finally* and replaced it with something that made more sense: *also*.

Also, a bride.

Finally, it all felt right.

Acknowledgments

The biggest moments in our lives can feel so secretly lonely, even when we're surrounded by the people we love. That's because we're always hiding a little bit of ourselves just in case we say too much, or become a little extra needy, or worse, we confess a little bit of doubt over what's supposed to be the happiest time in our lives. I've always found it settling being the most honest around the people I don't know. That honesty comes out only in my writing.

It took me five years to finish a book I originally started in 2019. I tried to finish it a thousand different times, and a thousand different times I said: *Later, tomorrow, next year, not now.* I wrote the final chapters last month, at 11 pm and 3 am and 4:15 am rocking Gemma to sleep during weeks long stretches of the most restless nights. Fighting brain fog and this intense desire to wait another year not writing this book, and feeling so sad about that, I'd type the pages in my head, put her down in her crib, whisper them over and over in my head, and pray I'd remember them in the morning.

Somehow I did. The pull to tell this story overcame tired eyes and self-doubt. I don't know if I have a million more days on this planet, or if I don't, but I do know this: *I am meant to write and tell stories.* I haven't been able to fully do that with this book lingering in my draft folder.

A special thank-you to the people who helped push me to publish this book.

My Monday morning newsletter crew. I never want to let you down.

Susan Shek for capturing the most important special moments of my life and letting me use them on book covers too.

Callie Walker for proofreading this book and chopping off all the overused grammar and spelling errors. Onur B. from Fiverr for designing the cover of this book and making that process seamless.

Adam, always. Gemma and Goofy, forever.

My own self for not letting seventeen rejection letters from publishers in 2019, a global pandemic, a new marriage, a new baby, and six full years of writing and not writing this book stop me from making it happen.

It's done. *Finally!* What will be next?

Love,

Jen Glantz

About the Author

Jen Glantz is the founder of Bridesmaid for Hire, the world's first company where strangers can hire a bridesmaid for their wedding. She's the author of "Always a Bridesmaid (for Hire)" and "All My Friends Are Engaged." Jen lives in Brooklyn with Adam (the husband), Gemma (the baby), and Goofy (the dog). She spends her free time eating slices of pizza and trying to figure out how to wear Forever 21 crop tops at the delightful age of thirty-six.

Say Hello to Jen Glantz
bridesmaidforhire.com
instagram.com/bridesmaidforhire
tiktok.com/@bridesmaidforhire
bridesmaidforhire.substack.com

www.ingramcontent.com/pod-product-compliance
Lightning Source LLC
Chambersburg PA
CBHW061322040426
42444CB00011B/2739